Invincible Investing: The Ultimate and Proven Investing Method of Principal Protection with Market Gains

Invincible Investing: The Ultimate and Proven Investing Method of Principal Protection with Market Gains

VANDERPAL METHOD®

Dr. Geoffrey VanderPal CFP®

© 2017 Dr. Geoffrey VanderPal CFP®
All rights reserved.

ISBN: 1546963626
ISBN 13: 9781546963622

Introduction

Just like there is no such thing as a free lunch, there is no such thing as a risk-free investment. The goal of the investor is to find a comfortable level of managed risk that provides the desired level of return.

The highest-return investments tend to have the highest level of risk, and the lowest-risk investments tend to have lowest returns. What if you could employ an investment method that provided a low level of managed risk and a relatively high return?

The goal of this book is to teach you how to achieve a higher-than-market return while preserving your capital. You will learn an easy-to-follow method that enables you to design your portfolio in a manner that takes little time and allows you to sleep at night.

The initial concepts are written in a basic concept form. After you learn the basics, you will build on this knowledge in a progressive manner to learn more advanced options that create greater flexibility and potentially higher returns. It is your choice whether to stick to the basics or learn more advanced trading techniques. If you are a novice, don't be intimidated by these few chapters. As the book progresses, so will the content and your knowledge.

My hope is that once you learn the VanderPal Method®, you will build a stable and profitabe portfolio for your future.

Geoffrey VanderPal, DBA, CFP®

Let's begin…

CHAPTER 1

THE TRUTH ABOUT RISK

Rule #1, don't lose the money. Rule #2, see rule #1.
—WARREN BUFFETT

In this chapter, you will learn about the risk factors of some common investment vehicles. You will discover that low risk is not no risk and that high risk can be managed risk.

The examples in this book will use a $10,000 investment and simplified explanations that ignore the rate of return reducing the drag of income taxes and brokerage fees. Before we delve into the material, imagine your current circumstances. More than likely you have lost money in the market or obtained very low returns. The investment and capital markets are a fickle beast, and as a small investor, it is difficult to truly understand the complicated and fast-paced world of trading and investment management. The purpose of this book it to provide a simplified and easy-to-read and easy-to-understand guide with no fluff, just the needed information and knowledge to use the VanderPal Method® and gain control of your money against loss and financial ruin. I have worked with thousands of clients as a financial adviser since 1994 when I began as a security-licensed registered representative at a major bank brokerage firm. In my humble beginnings, I came across many stories of how individual investors such as yourself were looking for higher returns without substantial risk. Back then I was a rookie and did not know much. I've since had years of working with clients and years of study, culminating in a doctorate and research and a dissertation exploring an idea that eventually became known as the VanderPal Method® of money management.

There were individuals such as Jacob (age 64) and Arlene (age 63) who were set to retire in 2008 until the housing and financial crisis occurred. In a few months, they had a home worth 40 percent less and a retirement portfolio that dropped 35 percent. There are countless stories such as these and some much worse. Every year for more than twenty-four years, a consulting firm named Dalbar has provided a report on the average returns and results for individual investors. Financial firms and advisers peruse the reports, and the results are nearly identical each year. The average individual investor earns a return on par with bank accounts' net of losses and fees. Clients who work with advisers on average fair better; however, there again are no guarantees. A 2014 published white paper from Vanguard stated that individual investors who invest with a professional adviser on average had a 3 percent annual increased return. Again, no guarantee of loss mitigation.

This book is not full stories to entertain. It is detailed, pertinent, and to the point. From this point onward, we will jump into the proverbial pool, and you will learn the techniques and methods of the VanderPal Method®. On the last few pages of the book, I have included a glossary of terms. Even though the terms are explained as you progress through the book, having access to a glossary to quickly look up words and their meanings will be more efficient.

Treasuries

US Treasury securities receive the backing of the full faith and credit of the US government. The Treasury's interest payments and repayment of principal are secured by the ability of the government to collect taxes, borrow money, or print money. Treasuries are the benchmark against which the risk factors of all other investments are measured. There are three main types of treasury securities: bills, notes, and bonds.

Treasury bills, known as *T-bills*, are short-duration debt obligations with a maximum maturity length of fifty-two weeks. The most common type of T-bills is ninety-one days in length. You give the government slightly less than the face value of the note, and it pays you the face value in ninety-one days. The difference is your interest payment.

Your capital is very safe, but the interest rate you receive is very low. It is this low interest rate that creates the risk of investing in T-bills. If you rolled over your investments three times, creating a total investment period of one year, you might receive interest at a rate of 0.5 percent on an annual basis. The problem is the silent killer of savings, inflation. If the inflation rate is 2 percent and you receive 0.5 percent interest, you have a loss of purchasing power of 1.5 percent per year.

Treasury notes have a longer time to maturity than T-bills with the five-year note being the most popular benchmark. With a five-year note, the US government guarantees you will receive your principal back at the end of the five-year period. However, you experience the same loss of purchasing power as with the T-bill. If you receive an interest rate of 1.5 percent per year and the inflation rate is 2 percent, you lose 0.5 percent each year for a total loss of purchasing power of 2.5 percent over five years. You also face the risk of having the market value of your five-year note decrease if market interest rates increase.

You have purchased a $10,000 five-year note with an interest rate of 1.5 percent, and over the course of the next year, the Federal Reserve raises interest rates by 1.5 percent, so that newly issued five-year bonds now pay 3 percent. You will still be entitled to $10,000 if you hold the five-year note for the final four years. However, if you need to sell the Note to raise cash, nobody is going to want to give you $10,000. To match the 3 percent interest rate investors receive purchasing new notes, you must sell your 1.5 percent note for a discounted price—in other words, at a loss.

Treasury bonds have maturity lengths of ten to thirty years, with the ten-year bond being the most common investment benchmark. Purchase a ten-year bond, and you should receive an interest rate close to the current rate of inflation. You will have a purchasing power loss only if inflation increases over the ten-year period. You will face the same risk of capital loss caused by rising interest rates as with the five-year note. There would be a chance that if interest rates were to decrease, you would have some capital appreciation. However, with interest rates near historic lows, the probability of increasing interest rates is much better than the probability of decreasing interest rates.

Bank Accounts

One of the safest places for your $10,000 is in a bank account. The Federal Deposit Insurance Corporation (FDIC) guarantees the return of your principal. The FDIC charges a premium to banks based on the size of their deposits. This money goes into a fund to pay back depositors in any bank that fails. If the insurance fund were to become depleted, the FDIC would simply look to the US Treasury Department for additional funds. Even during the 2008 financial crisis, no bank customers lost deposits covered by the insurance plan.

A bank money market keeps your money safe, but with a high 1 percent yield and a 2 percent inflation rate, you lose purchasing power at the rate of 1 percent per year. If market interest rates increase, the interest rate paid on your money market account (MMA) will increase.

A five-year certificate of deposit (CD) can pay an interest rate that matches the inflation rate. So, at the end of five years, you receive your money back and have lost no purchasing power. The catch is that taking your money out before the five-year period is over causes the bank greatly reducing your interest rate as a penalty, but you do receive all your principal back even if interest rates have increased.

Annuities

Annuities are investment contracts offered by insurance companies. Annuities come in two main types, fixed and variable. Annuities also offer tax-deferral in nonqualified or nonretirement accounts.

Fixed annuities set the payment amount like an interest rate and guarantee the value of your principal. What the insurance company is doing is taking your capital and invest in bonds, equities, and real estate. The company pays you a relatively low rate of return and keeps all the profits above that rate. Most annuities also have surrender charges if you take money out of the annuity in the first few years of ownership. Fixed annuity principal guarantees are only as good as the insurance company issuing the policy. Fixed annuities are not a good place to keep your liquid cash or seek decent investment returns.

There is a hybrid version of a fixed annuity known as *equity index annuities*. These contracts invest money into bonds and index options and provide a percentage or portion of the upside of the index return to the annuity contract owner while profiting the remainder return. The basis of the VanderPal Method® was based upon this very concept. The difference being that you can create your own version with greater potential returns, less fees, no sales commissions and greater flexibility.

Variable annuities do not pay a set return or guarantee the value of your principal. You can choose from a number different investment funds in which you can place your money. These funds primarily invest in stocks and bonds with you getting the profits from investing after paying asset management fees and mortality expense that can range from 2 percent to 3.5 percent per annum.

In a bad market year, the value of your variable annuity fund will drop along with the market plus an additional 2–3.5 percent for the fees. Some companies do offer policies that protect you against these losses. One type of policy indemnifies you against any losses in return for controlling how your funds are allocated in the annuity and of course there are additional fees.

Another type of policy insurers your principal against loss by charging you a portfolio protection insurance premium that can range from 1.5 percent to 5 percent of the principal value of your account. You pay that premium every year on the rising value of your account in addition to the asset management fees.

Variable annuities tend to have higher sales and surrender charges than fixed annuities. These annuities are neither a great place to keep your cash or a source of good investment returns.

Mutual Funds

Mutual funds are registered investment companies that sell shares to individual investors and pool the money raised into a portfolio of investments per the stated objective of the fund. The most common types of securities held in mutual fund portfolios are investment-grade bonds and common stocks.

Bond funds have the similar risk factors as Treasury securities. Short-term bond funds will have trouble providing returns exceeding the rate of inflation, and long-term bond funds will be susceptible to reduction of principal due to increasing interest rates. Corporate bond funds also face the additional risk of principal loss if a company finds itself in financial trouble and defaults on its debt obligations. The advantage of a bond fund is diversification and lowering the impact of default and credit risk.

Stock funds invest in the publicly traded common stock of corporations. An investment in stock funds will go up and down with the fortunes of the individual stocks owned in the portfolio and the fate of the general market. There are two types of stock fund management, active and passive.

An actively managed fund has portfolio managers and researchers who attempt to pick winning stocks to invest in and losing stocks to avoid. The problem with actively managed funds is that while a few fund managers have extended periods of winning records, most actively managed funds do not provide returns that exceed those of benchmark stock market indexes such as the Standard & Poor's 500 (S&P 500) Index. The lack of market beating performance is the cause for the rising popularity of passive funds.

Passively managed funds, also known as *index funds*, do not have fund managers or researchers trying to pick stocks. Passive funds typically invest your money in all the stocks contained in a broad market benchmark such as the S&P 500 Index. Funds will buy all five hundred stocks in the index in direct correlation to each stock's weighting within the index. Your investment returns are at the whim of the stock market. If the market goes up, you make money, and if the market goes down, you lose money. If the market goes down as it did in the dot-com bust and the 2008 financial crisis, you can lose much money. Remember, when an investment goes down 50 percent, it has to rise 100 percent to return to the original value.

Long-term investors in passive funds, ignoring the short-term ups and downs of the market, benefit from the tendency of the market to rise over the long term. The problem for the long-term investor is that while the returns over extended periods of time tend to be positive, they are very vanilla. There is no reason to expect returns that exceed the growth rate in the gross domestic product (GDP) plus the inflation rate added to dividend payouts. If GDP growth rate is 3.5 percent, the inflation rate is 3 percent, and if dividend payouts are 2.25 percent, the base rate of return is 8.75 percent. After subtracting management expense ratio of 0.25 percent, the real return after adjusting for inflation is only 5.5 percent.

Stocks

Stocks need little explaining. When you buy a share of common stock, you own a small piece of the company and the right to receive any dividends paid. If the stock goes up in price, you make money, and if the stock declines, you suffer a loss.

You decide to invest in Apple Inc. (AAPL) because you love your new iPhone. You buy one hundred shares at $100 per share for a total of $10,000. If the stock goes up 20 percent over the next year, you turn a profit of $2,000 plus $200 in dividends for a total of $2,200. If the stock goes down 20 percent, you lose $2,000 less $200 in dividends for a total loss of $1,800. It's the full joy or the full pain of complete risk exposure.

You can attempt to limit your losses by using stop loss orders. You bought the stock at $100 figuring if it drops to $90, you made the wrong choice. So, you place a stop order to sell if the price hits $90. When the stock trades at $90, your shares are sold at market price, limiting your losses if the stock continues to fall. Of course, if the stock rebounds and goes higher, you have given up the chance to make a profit.

Exchange-Traded Funds

The simplest explanation of exchange-traded funds (ETFs) is that they are like passively managed mutual funds that trade on the stock exchange. You purchase mutual funds directly from the asset management fund company or through a stockbroker, at a price set at the close of the market each day. You buy or sell ETFs through a stockbroker. ETFs are highly liquid. You may trade ETFs at any time during market hours.

Trading ETFs exposes you to the same open risks as trading stocks with the exception that you have no exposure to the risk of negative news about one company. The most highly traded ETF, the SPDR S&P 500 ETF (SPY), spreads your exposure across all 500 stocks making up the index essentially limiting you to generic market risk.

Stock Options

A stock option is a contract that gives you the right to buy or sell the underlying stock, and for this right you pay a per-share fee called a *premium*. Options trade on the exchanges like stocks. The right to buy the stock is a *call option*. The right to sell is a *put option*.

Confused? Here is an example using AAPL.

You believe that the release of Apple Inc.'s newest gadget—an implantable virtual reality device—is going to drive up the stock price within the next three months. You can buy one hundred shares at $100 for a total investment of $10,000. If the release causes the stock to rise to $110, you can sell for a $1,000 profit. You have received a return on investment of 10 percent. If you're wrong and the share price drops to $90, you lose $1,000.

Instead of buying the actual stock, you could buy a call option that expires in ninety days. You buy one option that allows you to buy one hundred shares of AAPL any time during the next ninety days for $100 per share. The premium established by the market is $2 per share. You need to put up only $200 per contract ($2 premium times one hundred shares for a contract) instead of $10,000 to buy the stock.

People love the new gizmo, and AAPL stock is trading at $110. You close out your position with a profit of $1,000 minus the $200 premium for a net profit of $800, representing an 8 percent profit on the $10,000 capital you could have invested in the stock or an $800 return on a $200 premium, which is a 400 percent return.

The power of options comes from the leveraged return on the premiums paid. In this example, you paid a $200 premium to receive an $800 profit for return on capital placed at risk of 100 percent. The entire time you were a holder of the call option, you never had more than $200 at risk. This is why the actual return is 400 percent.

Options are a great tool for creating acceptable levels of managed risk. If the share price had dropped to $90, you would not have lost $1,000 as you would have when owning the stock. Even if the stock plummeted to $70 per share, you would have been out only $200.

Options are not available for all stocks, and it is best to stay with options that have enough trading volume to ensure liquidity. Stocks are not the only investments that have options. There are also options available for many ETFs, stock indexes, and commodities.

How do you make this information work for you?

Read the next section on the VanderPal Method® to find out.

Exchange-Traded Funds

The simplest explanation of exchange-traded funds (ETFs) is that they are like passively managed mutual funds that trade on the stock exchange. You purchase mutual funds directly from the asset management fund company or through a stockbroker, at a price set at the close of the market each day. You buy or sell ETFs through a stockbroker. ETFs are highly liquid. You may trade ETFs at any time during market hours.

Trading ETFs exposes you to the same open risks as trading stocks with the exception that you have no exposure to the risk of negative news about one company. The most highly traded ETF, the SPDR S&P 500 ETF (SPY), spreads your exposure across all 500 stocks making up the index essentially limiting you to generic market risk.

Stock Options

A stock option is a contract that gives you the right to buy or sell the underlying stock, and for this right you pay a per-share fee called a *premium*. Options trade on the exchanges like stocks. The right to buy the stock is a *call option*. The right to sell is a *put option*.

Confused? Here is an example using AAPL.

You believe that the release of Apple Inc.'s newest gadget—an implantable virtual reality device—is going to drive up the stock price within the next three months. You can buy one hundred shares at $100 for a total investment of $10,000. If the release causes the stock to rise to $110, you can sell for a $1,000 profit. You have received a return on investment of 10 percent. If you're wrong and the share price drops to $90, you lose $1,000.

Instead of buying the actual stock, you could buy a call option that expires in ninety days. You buy one option that allows you to buy one hundred shares of AAPL any time during the next ninety days for $100 per share. The premium established by the market is $2 per share. You need to put up only $200 per contract ($2 premium times one hundred shares for a contract) instead of $10,000 to buy the stock.

People love the new gizmo, and AAPL stock is trading at $110. You close out your position with a profit of $1,000 minus the $200 premium for a net profit of $800, representing an 8 percent profit on the $10,000 capital you could have invested in the stock or an $800 return on a $200 premium, which is a 400 percent return.

The power of options comes from the leveraged return on the premiums paid. In this example, you paid a $200 premium to receive an $800 profit for return on capital placed at risk of 100 percent. The entire time you were a holder of the call option, you never had more than $200 at risk. This is why the actual return is 400 percent.

Options are a great tool for creating acceptable levels of managed risk. If the share price had dropped to $90, you would not have lost $1,000 as you would have when owning the stock. Even if the stock plummeted to $70 per share, you would have been out only $200.

Options are not available for all stocks, and it is best to stay with options that have enough trading volume to ensure liquidity. Stocks are not the only investments that have options. There are also options available for many ETFs, stock indexes, and commodities.

How do you make this information work for you?

Read the next section on the VanderPal Method® to find out.

CHAPTER 2

INTRODUCTION TO THE VANDERPAL METHOD®

The Vanderpal Method® enables you to receive capital gains in upward- or downward-moving markets while protecting up to 100 percent of your principal in FDIC-insured bank accounts, short-term US government bonds, or other stable underlying assets. Over time, the gains earned and recognized from market participation are reinvested back into the principal amount maintained in FDIC-insured banks or short-term US government bonds. The method creates a ratchet effect, locking in gains to provide increasing principal value. This program allows for significant principal preservation, the liquidity of funds, and participation in the gains of more than one thousand stocks and dozens of indices.

The Vanderpal Method® has lower risk and volatility factors than most investment methods. A later chapter will discuss the details. Now you will be taken through a basic example of how the Vanderpal Method® works. The case assumes a capital balance of $100,000. Do not worry if you have less capital as the method applies to you, but round numbers make for a clearer illustration.

CYA

The first principal of the VanderPal Method® adheres to rule #1. You deposit your principal in an interest-bearing bank account. You can choose between MMAs and higher-yielding CD or a mixture of the two. The choice depends on your needs for liquidity. Longer-term accounts will pay a higher rate of interest to reinvest into the program.

Ideally, only your interest is used to fund the trading account, but at the beginning, a small percentage of principal is required to prime the pump. The goal is to keep this percentage below 5 percent for limiting principal risk. Where do you invest these funds?

Long-Term Equity Anticipation Securities

The previous discussion of stock options used the example of an option on AAPL that expired in ninety days. Most options expire in a relatively short period, but one type lasts longer.

Long-Term Equity Anticipation Securities (LEAPS) are special long-term options that expire in select months and can have a duration of up to three years. LEAPS options represent one hundred shares and trade just like regular options. LEAPS equity options allow you to profit from the long-term growth of a company without having to make a large investment in a company's stock. LEAPS index options allow you to profit from the growth of a single economic sector or the entire market. Some popularly traded ETFs also have long-term options.

Illustration

You have a firm belief that the economic outlook is improving and the stock market will experience solid growth over the next two years. You could invest in one hundred shares of the SPY at

$200 per share for a total of $20,000. You are putting 100 percent of your capital fully at risk.

If the market rises 20 percent, you make a profit of $4,000, and if it falls 20 percent, you lose $4,000.

Using the VanderPal Method®, you purchase a long-term $200 call option that expires in one year. The option premium is $800. The market rises 20 percent, and you make a $4,000 profit minus the premium of $800 for a net profit of $3,200. No matter how much the market falls, you can never lose more than the $800 premium. A 16 percent return upon the notional portfolio value of $20,000 or a 400 percent return based upon the premium versus return. Keep in mind that longer-term options such as LEAPS do have higher premiums to compensate for the longer time periods in which the contract holder can participate. The idea is to generate enough interest growth to pay for most or all of the option premium. In other words, the premium is primarily paid for by interest or dividends of the underlying safe investments in the principal account.

Ratcheting

Ratcheting is the process of growing both the principal account and the investment account simultaneously over time. The increase in both accounts is important, but there is an ongoing conflict between the desire for a higher rate of return and a growing pool of safe principal. Exactly how to achieve a balance between the two objectives depends on your tolerance for risk and investment goals.

The VanderPal Method® is a long-term investment strategy. Here is a common long-term scenario.

When you begin, you are putting only 2–5 percent of portfolio capital at risk. This is a nice comfortable risk point, but you are purchasing only one or two investment contracts, which boost the portfolio profits above the mere interest rate of return but are not at the market-beating level you want to achieve.

Look at the first few investment periods like driving up the entrance ramp to the freeway. You want to accelerate return. During this period, you want to increase the number of contracts you hold in a low-risk manner. The best way to accomplish this is to add all interest income to the investment account with all profits from the investment account put into the principal account. Given the current low interest rate environment, you might consider reinvesting part of the profits or choosing a different type of principal investment with a higher yield. The full discussion of your options is in a later chapter.

Once you have built the investment account to three times its initial size, you can consider yourself merged on to the freeway and ready to cruise.

Now that you are cruising down the road, it is time to audit your situation and your goals. Obviously, the path to the greatest total returns is to continue to invest all interest and some profits into more contracts. However, a central concept of the VanderPal Method® is that you become a rational and intelligent investor who realizes that profits are not entirely real until you take your chips off the table, cash them in, and add the proceeds to your safe principal account.

The rational choice at this stage of cruising along is where you keep reinvesting the interest payments in the principal account and return a larger portion of investment profits to the principal account if you made a choice to reinvest some profits. Depending on your current rate of portfolio return, you might be ready for the final stage.

The final stage is cruising down the highway on a beautiful day with the top down. You stop reinvesting any of the investment profits back into the portfolio and place all the money into your principal account.

Thoughts on Portfolio Size

The illustration in this chapter uses a portfolio size of $100,000 because this is the point where the percentage of the portfolio at risk on one S&P 500 SPY option hits the sweet spot. You can use the SPY options with a smaller portfolio with the realization that you are risking a higher percentage of your capital. A $1,000 option premium would be 5 percent of a $20,000 portfolio. To have parity and match index returns, one can take the option contract value and divide it into the amount of the safe portfolio to determine how many contracts to have 100 percent or near 100 percent participation. Take the strike price of a contract, multiply it by the multiplier, and this will provide the notional or contract value that can then be divided into principal or safe account value. More will be discussed later as to the actual calculation of an example.

You do have other investment choices such as LEAPS of blue-chip companies that have a beta of less than one and contracts that require a lower commitment of principal. A stocks beta is a measure of how it tends to perform in relation to the overall market. A stock with a beta of one would rise 1 percent when the market rises 1 percent and fall 1 percent when the market falls 1 percent. The reason for using only large-cap stocks with a beta of less than one is the VanderPal Method® focus on reduced risk and volatility. A stock with a beta of 0.8 would show a 20 percent reduction in volatility to market risk compared with the S&P 500 Index. Your investment choices are part of a later section on investment alternatives.

CHAPTER 3

THE PRINCIPAL BUCKET

The Principal Bucket is the place to keep your capital nice and safe while receiving a steady interest return to invest into the VanderPal Method®. The purest form of the method keeps your money in the safest possible investment choices.

Today's unnatural low interest rate environment favors borrowers over savers. You might consider taking on a little bit more manageable risk to boost your cash flow for reinvestment. This chapter covers your easiest and lowest-risk alternatives first, then continues to higher-risk income investments with a discussion on the risk and rewards of each.

Bank Accounts

The FDIC guarantees your deposit in any one bank account up to $250,000. A reserve fund of premiums collected for member banks is the technical backing for the insurance. The reality is that the US government will cover any FDIC obligations if the reserve fund was used up, as not to do so would lead to the collapse of our entire economic system. Your principal is safe.

The downside to bank accounts is that current interest rates are low.

Some banks are paying 1 percent on MMAs, but your local bank might pay as low as 0.1 percent. MMAs have the advantage that when the Federal Reserve raises interest rates, banks will usually raise your interest rate accordingly.

Bank CDs pay slightly higher rates of interest in exchange for your guaranteeing to keep the money in the account for the specified length of time. The interest rates are slightly higher, but you must commit to three years to get 1.5 percent and five years to receive 2 percent. When the Fed increases interest rates, your interest rate will not go up. You must wait until the end of the CD period to obtain a higher rate. You can access sites such as Bankrate.com to search for the highest CD rates in the United States.

There are two forces destroying your real returns on bank accounts. The interest income received is fully taxable, which reduces your actual return by your marginal tax rate. At a 2 percent rate of inflation, your after-tax purchasing power is reduced by approximately 1 percent.

US Treasuries

US Treasury securities are the debt instruments issued by the US government to pay the portion of its bills that are not covered by income-tax revenues. Treasury securities are the benchmark security for measuring the risk factors of all other debt instruments. If the US government cannot manage ongoing interest payments and repayment of principal, all money is essentially worthless.

The price of investing in such highly rated securities is that the interest rates are low. Committing your capital for five years pays you just less than the estimated 2 percent inflation rate. You need to buy the ten-year bond before receiving a return greater than the rate of inflation.

Interest payments from treasuries are subject to federal taxation, but you do not have to pay state income taxes on the money you earn. The tax burden assures that you will lose purchasing power to inflation. However, your principal is very safe, and you will soon learn how to make inflation-beating profits.

Zero-Coupon Bonds

A zero-coupon bond does not pay periodic interest payments. Earnings accumulate over the life of the bond and represent the difference between a deeply discounted purchase price and the bond's face value at maturity. US Treasury securities are the basis for the safest form of a zero-coupon bond.

The bonds are created by separating the interest payments from the principal of underlying bond through a process called *coupon stripping*. The securities are then sold in two pieces. One investor gets the interest payments, and the other investor purchases the bond at a discounted price set using prevailing interest rates. The purchaser of the zero-coupon bond receives the bond's full face value on its maturity date.

Zero-coupon treasuries were created by investment banks and were so popular that the Treasury Department created its version called *STRIPs*. The cost of purchasing $100,000 worth of STRIPs maturing in five years is slightly more than $90,000. You give the Treasury Department $90,000 now, and it gives you $100,000 in five years. You would pay approximately $78,000 for STRIPs worth $100,000 in ten years. The difference is capital you can use to fund the VanderPal Method®.

There is a very active secondary market for the trading of zero-coupon bonds providing you with reasonable liquidity.

However, if interest rates go up, you would experience some capital loss. It is best only to commit funds to the purchasing of zero-coupon bonds that you do not anticipate needing before the bonds mature.

Again, there is the nagging problem of federal taxation. You are required to report the phantom interest you are not receiving on your annual tax returns. You are still not beating inflation on an after-tax basis. If you wish to receive higher returns, you will need to take on a slightly higher amount of risk.

Government Agency Securities

The Treasury Department is not the only issuer of government securities. A few government agencies such as the Small Business Administration (SBA) and the Government National Mortgage Association (Ginnie Mae) also issue securities. Ginnie Mae issues mortgage-backed securities (MBS) based on first mortgage loans issued or insured by the Department of Veterans Affairs (VA), the Rural Housing Service (RHS), or Federal Housing Administration (FHA). The mortgages are to first-time homeowners of moderate income who are required to make down payments of 5 percent or less. Ginnie Mae pools together mortgages issued at the same mortgage rate and by a single approved lender into individual MBSs called *GNMAs*.

GNMAs are not the low-down-payment, negative-amortization, no-income-verification, subprime-loan securities made infamous during the 2008 financial crisis. Banks certified to issue the loans must adhere to rigorous underwriting standards, and homes undergo extensive appraisals performed by a select group of approved licensed appraisers. The tight underwriting standards are designed to minimize default risk.

Due to the lower default risk and the government's desire to encourage first-time homeownership, principal and interest payments are fully insured by Ginnie Mae. While Ginnie Mae does charge a small fee for this insurance, the principal and interest payments on GNMAs are backed by the full faith and credit of the US government. The guarantee places GNMAs at the same ultra-low risk level of Treasury securities.

GNMAs are subject to the same risk of changing interest rates as are Treasury securities. Due to two other risk factors, GNMAs pay slightly higher interest rates than Treasuries. The interest income from GNMAs is fully taxable and not exempt from state income taxes. The higher interest rates are also compensation for prepayment risk.

Part of every loan payment is a partial principal payment. Borrowers may pay off the loans early for reasons such as selling the home or mortgage refinancing, resulting in the return of principal to investors in MBSs. The uncertainty of when prepayments will occur and at what interest rate the principal receives on reinvestment is the prepayment risk. Prepayments are not necessarily bad. During a period of rising interest rates, reinvested funds get a higher rate of return. Prepayments usually go down during periods of rising interest rates as refinancing is not to the benefit of the borrowers.

Individual GNMAs are available for purchase in par value amounts of $25,000. An active secondary market allows you to pick the length of time to the maturity of your GNMAs. Remember that the closer an MBS is to maturity, the greater the proportion of principal to interest in each payment. This is a good thing during rising interest rate periods and a bad thing when interest rates are falling.

You do not need to buy individual securities to invest in GNMAs as ETFs are an available option. The popular iShares GNMA bond ETF (NASDAQ: GNMA) diversifies your investment across a vast array of GNMAs with different maturity dates and coupon payments, which reduce your overall risk. You get a yield of about 2 percent while paying a low expense fee of 0.15 percent. GNMAs lend themselves to active management and market timing by bond experts. Facing the specter of rising interest rates, the fund is keeping a cash position of more than 40 percent invested in very short-term government securities. The cash can be invested in GNMAs as rates increase, and the liquidity enables the fund to handle any redemptions without the need to liquidate current holdings.

Another diversification option is to use a low-fee, open-ended mutual fund. The Vanguard GNMA Fund (VFIJX) charges an expense fee of only 0.11 percent and has an SEC yield of slightly over 2 percent. Fund managers control interest rate risk by investing primarily in intermediate-term securities and currently have the average maturity of the portfolio at less than six years. Newly issued MBS have a period to maturity of thirty years.

Corporate Bond Funds

A step up in both returns and risks are investment-grade corporate bonds. Investment-grade bonds receive a score from rating services, such as Moody's Investor Services, Fitch Ratings, or S&P's Ratings Services, of AAA, AA, or A. Some asset managers include BBB-rated bonds as investment grade.

Buying individual corporate bonds exposes you to the default risk of a single corporation. Funds spread capital between hundreds of different securities, eliminating most default risk. If one company cannot pay, it represents just a small portion of the fund's capital.

There is credit rate risk with a corporate bond fund. If interest rates increase, the value of the bonds in the fund decreases, though they do keep paying the same interest rate. Conversely, if interest rates decrease, the value of the bonds increases. The bond value fluctuations should not bother you, as both you and fund management are long-term investors.

While you might experience a minor decrease in capital when interest rates increase, new money invested into the fund is purchasing bonds based on the new interest rates. The new bonds in the portfolio increase the yield on your investment. As previously purchased bonds mature, the full-face value goes back to the fund, which invests in new bonds at the higher interest rates, further increasing your yield. Eventually, the entire portfolio will mature and get reinvested at higher rates.

Corporate bond funds have different investment styles, of which the main three are short-term funds, intermediate-term funds, and long-term funds. Long-term bond funds take too long to turn over and refresh the portfolio, increasing the interest rate risk. Given the potential probability of the Federal Reserve increasing short-term interest rates, you are safer sticking to investments in short-term or intermediate-term funds. The short-term fund will refresh its portfolio completely in about two and a half years, and the intermediate-term fund will refresh its portfolio over about five years.

You can use either ETFs or mutual funds. You will pay commissions when initially purchasing ETF shares and when adding money to your principal bucket. You should not pay any transaction fees when using mutual funds. What is very important in the current low interest rate environment is to avoid funds with high expense ratios, as the expense ratio eats directly into your yield.

Vanguard Group is a mutually owned company known for its low expense fees. It offers short-term and intermediate-term corporate bond funds in both ETF and mutual fund formats that charge an ultra-low expense fee of only 0.1 percent. The mutual funds are no-load with no sales charges, redemption charges, or embedded marketing fees of any kind. The fee structure is so low due to Vanguard's corporate structure, which makes investors in its funds the owners of the funds, and the funds, in turn, own the company. All the money that would normally be profit to an asset manager is given back to investors in the form of lower fees. You do not need to use a fund from Vanguard but should use the funds as benchmarks to judge any other funds you are considering.

What kind of returns can you expect? Using comparable standards to the interest rate information for bank accounts and treasuries, you could expect to receive 1.5–2 percent from a short-term fund and 2.5–3 percent from an intermediate-term fund. You now stand a better chance of matching inflation. Unfortunately, corporate bond interest is fully taxable. Your after-tax return is at best even with inflation or slightly below. You might want to look at removing the taxable income factor.

Municipal Bond Funds

Municipal bond funds invest in the debt obligations of state governments, counties, cities, school districts, and related local government agencies. Interest payments on the securities issued by these entities have the benefit of being exempt from federal income taxation. A 1 percent tax-exempt return on a short-term municipal bond fund equates to 1.2 percent for someone in the 15 percent marginal federal bracket and 1.6 percent for someone who pays the top marginal bracket of 39.6 percent. An intermediate return of 1.75 percent equals 2.05 percent or 3 percent to the same taxpayers. You have a chance of matching inflation or maybe even exceeding the inflation rate depending on your tax bracket.

You want to put your money only in funds that invest solely in investment-grade bonds and have low expense ratios. Vanguard has a couple of good funds that you can use as benchmarks. ETFs have an advantage of providing intraday liquidity, but mutual funds provide daily liquidity, which is sufficient for your status as a long-term investor. ETFs allow you to use stop/loss orders as automatic protection from a rapid rise in interest rates, while mutual funds require you to approve any liquidation.

Senior Loan Funds

Senior loans are corporate bank loans sold on the secondary market. The term *senior* refers to the fact that the loan holders are first in line to get paid. Companies often put up their assets such as real estate, inventory, and intellectual property as security for the loans.

The companies receiving the loans are usually not investment-grade firms. Most loans in the fund portfolios are to firms within the B credit score ratings. This implies a higher default risk, which is greatly reduced by the senior positioning. Investors in the loans come before subordinated debt holders, bond holders, owners of preferred stock, and common stock investors. Typically, 80 percent of funds are collected from loans that go into total default and liquidation. Borrowers pay back the vast majority of loans as agreed.

Senior loans face a reduced risk from increasing interest rates as they have floating rate coupons. The loans have interest rate reset dates that are usually quarterly. If market interest rates rise, the rate on the loans increases by a proportional amount. Your yield will automatically benefit from Federal Reserve rate increases. The rate adjustability and the loans' average maturity age of about five years provide the added benefit of reducing price volatility compared with bond funds.

ETFs are the best choice for investing in senior loans. Two of the largest funds are the PowerShares Senior Loan Portfolio ETF (NYSEArca: BLKN) and SPDR Blackstone/GSO Senior Loan ETF (NYSEArca: SRLN). The funds track similar loan indexes but invest differently. The Senior Loan Portfolio ETF invests directly in loans included in its tracking index, while the GSO Senior Loan ETF invests indirectly through a master trust run by the primary investment manager, State Street Global Advisors. The master trust manages senior loan portfolios for all of State Street's funds and clients.

Numerous asset managers offer floating-rate-loan open-ended mutual funds. Fidelity Investments' highly rated Fidelity Floating Rate High Income Fund (FFRHX) is one of the few no-load choices. The fund does have a 1 percent short-term redemption fee imposed on shares held for less than sixty days. You, the long-term investor, have protection from volatility caused by people engaged in mutual fund trading as opposed to investing.

Floating-rate loan funds do charge higher expense fees. Expect to pay between 0.5 percent and 0.8 percent. Higher yields offset the higher expenses. Expect to receive yields after expenses of 3–4 percent.

High-Yield Corporate Bonds

Occupying the next step up the risk/return ladder is high-yield corporate bonds. These are the bonds of companies that are below investment grade and therefore need to carry a higher rate of interest to attract investors. These bonds are known as *junk bonds*. High-yield bonds are a good way to diversify risk and boost portfolio returns. The bonds are riskier than treasuries but historically have higher returns.

Investing in individual high-yield bonds is a time-consuming endeavor and best left to professional money managers. There are plenty of ETFs and mutual funds available.

An ETF example is the iShares iBoxx $ High Yield Corporate Bond (NYSEArca: HYG). HYG tracks the Markit iBoxx USD Liquid High Yield Index by investing in the bonds comprising the index. Its goal is to provide a higher yield with manageable risk and volatility. The fund has an SEC yield of 5.22 percent, an expense ratio of 0.49 percent, and an equity beta of 0.44. A securities beta measures how volatile its pricing is in relation to the broader stock market. A security with a beta of one would tend to increase 1 percent when the market increases 1 percent and fall 1 percent when the market decreases 1 percent. Very few stocks have a beta as low as 0.44.

Vanguard offers the no-load Vanguard High-Yield Corporate Fund. The fund invests in a portfolio of more than four hundred fifty medium-quality bonds seeking to provide consistent income while minimizing defaults and potential of principal loss. The fund charges an expense fee of only 0.13 percent and has an SEC yield of more than 4.8 percent.

There are many ETFs and mutual funds from which to choose. Remember that even in junk bonds, quality does matter. All funds have charts that show the portfolio distribution sorted by underlying security risk. You want a fund that has a good distribution within the B range of securities with almost no exposure to C rated bonds or below. The lower-grade securities have higher yields that come with an unacceptably high risk of default.

Preferred Stock

You are probably familiar with common stock, which gives you an ownership stake in a company. Common stock comes with voting rights and often a dividend payment. Preferred stock is different.

Preferred stock is a hybrid security. It is an equity security that acts like a bond. Similar to common stocks, preferred stocks trade on an exchange and have daily liquidity. The preferred part of the stock is that the holder of preferred stock has a claim on the company's income and assets that is superior to that of the owners of common stock. Companies must pay the dividends on preferred stock in full before they can pay a dividend on the common stock.

Like a bond, preferred stock issues have a par value. The par value is usually $1,000 or $25. The stock has a set dividend payment like the interest rate on a bond. Stockholders receive dividend payments on a quarterly basis.

Preferred stock has no voting rights and lacks the upside potential of common stock, as preferred stock pricing fluctuates per the relationship between the dividend rate in relation to the face value of the stock. The stock is usually issued callable at face value on or after a specific date in the future, allowing the company to repurchase the shares at par value if it believes that it can easily raise money at a better rate. The share prices of preferred stock can fluctuate with interest rates like a bond does.

The small downsides of preferred stock are made up for by the upside. The upside is that the dividend rates are generous. It is easy to find preferred issues paying between 4.5 percent and 9 percent. The companies issuing preferred stock include some large financially stable organizations that have very little chance of not meeting their dividend obligations. The market price of preferred stock will fluctuate some based upon market influences but generally much less than common stock.

Companies such as Pacific Gas & Electric, Wells Fargo, J.P. Morgan, and General Electric have outstanding preferred stock. The issues of these four companies pay dividends ranging from 4.75 percent to 6 percent. You can easily find six to sixteen other high-quality companies and build your portfolio. If you do not desire to manage a portfolio of preferred stocks, there are fund options available.

Only a small number of mutual funds are dedicated to preferred stocks, though many high-income funds invest in preferred stocks. The problem with the dedicated mutual funds is that they charge an up-front fee to purchase the funds. You could pay a sales charge of 2.75 percent, or you can keep the 2.75 percent and invest in a good preferred stock ETF.

The iShares US Preferred Stock ETF (NYSEArca: PFF) tracks the S&P US Preferred Stock Index by investing in the approximately three hundred securities making up the index in direct proportion to their weighting in the index, providing significant diversification against default risk. The fund charges an expense fee of 0.47 percent, has an equity beta of 0.32, and has an SEC yield of almost 5.5 percent. You do have exposure to a degree of interest rate risk, but there is a fund for that.

The PowerShares Variable Rate Preferred Portfolio ETF (NYSEArca: VRP) tracks the Wells Fargo Hybrid and Preferred Securities Floating and Variable Rate Index. The index consists of hybrid securities that have a variable or floating-rate payment. Both the index and the fund rebalance securities weighting every month.

The advantage of the VRP is that if interest rates rise, the payments will rise on reset dates, which are either quarterly or annually depending on the original prospectus of the underlying security. The fund has an SEC yield of 5 percent and expense fee of 0.5 percent.

That is the extent of fixed-income securities. There are some types of equity-based securities that have higher yields, but they involve market risk factors that make them unsuitable for the principal bucket.

On to an investment opportunity that is new to most people.

Peer-to-Peer Lending

An interesting new way to receive returns that are higher than market rate comes from the financial technology industry and is called *peer-to-peer lending*. Peer-to-peer (P2P) lending is a system that matches consumer borrowers with investors who fund the loans. It is not as sketchy as it sounds. Top providers, such as Lending Club and Prosper, arrange billions of dollars of loans per year.

Borrowers looking to refinance credit card debt, buy a car, fund a vacation, or cover any other personal loan purpose apply through the P2P platform provider. The platform provider turns the application over to a bank that checks the credit scores and financial data of the borrower. If the borrower's information is good, the loan is approved at an interest rate commensurate with the borrower's credit worthiness. If the borrower accepts the interest rate and conditions of the loan, the loan is uploaded to the lending platform, where independent investors can choose to fund the loan in return for receiving the interest and principal payments. Platforms charge about 1 percent of the interest and principal payments as their compensation.

P2P lending is a winning situation for everybody. The bank involved in the processing and the initial issuing of the loan receives a small but highly profitable fee for the short period it is involved in the process. The financial technology company running the platform receives its ongoing fees and extra fees if it is required to collect from delinquent borrowers.

The borrower receives a loan up to $35,000 at interest rates between 7 percent and 26 percent. The interest rates are lower than what they would pay to a traditional finance company or lender. High-credit-quality borrowers often receive interest rates below those credit union members would pay. It's an all-around good deal for the borrower.

The biggest winners in P2P lending are the investors. Investors receive the interest and principal payments of the borrowers minus the fees paid to the platform provider and the bank. Investors do have exposure to default risk, but the lending platform provides a way to diversify the risk.

An investor is not required to invest a large amount in any single loan or to invest in high-credit-risk loans. Investments as low as $25 into each loan are available. A $2,500 account might have an interest in as many as one hundred loans, creating a highly diversified portfolio with little risk of default losses from any one loan. Diversified loan portfolios have a more than 99 percent record of profitability.

Investors can set the account to invest in whatever level of credit risk they desire. Conservative investors choosing to invest in the highest-quality loan categories can expect to receive a yield of around 6 percent, which is a very good yield in the current income investment climate. Loan proceeds can be accumulated or reinvested into new loans. If interest rates rise, the reinvestments will go into loans paying a higher rate of return. VanderPal Method® investors can use the returns to fund their participation accounts.

Every investment has its downsides. Investors in P2P loans could experience higher default rates if the economy were to head into a strong recession. There is also a loss of liquidity. There is not a secondary market for loan portfolios. The typical loan is three to five years in length, and you will not receive your money back until the borrower fully pays off the loan. The commitment is not a problem for the long-term investor, but P2P lending is not a place to put cash reserves.

Interest payments are still fully taxable. The difference is with P2P lending, you are finally getting an after-tax return that beats inflation.

P2P lending is a rapidly expanding business. The returns are attractive enough that private investment pools are joining individual investors as participants in funding loans.

Making Your Investment Choice

Using the purest and simplest method of the VanderPal Method®, you put your principal into one bucket using either bank accounts or Treasury securities as the funding vehicle and placing the interest you receive each year into your participation bucket. A central VanderPal Method® theme is "safety first, last, and always."

The challenge is that the current interest rates are below the ideal level needed to receive full market participation. This requires some adjustments and choices until the rates rise to more historically normal levels of 4.5 percent or higher. The higher return and risk investments are good as part of a diversified portfolio but not meant to be the base of a secure portfolio.

The first choice is to determine what you consider to be an acceptable level of risk. If you are extremely concerned with the safety of principal, use bank accounts and treasuries. If you are comfortable taking on a little more short-term risk, choose between the short-term bond funds based on your tax bracket. If two- to five-year value fluctuations do not bother you, you may move up to the intermediate-term bond funds, preferred stock funds, and senior floating rate funds. Some corporate long-term bond funds do have high enough yields, but your long-term interests are better served by avoiding them and making other choices.

If you want even higher returns and are not averse to more risk, give P2P lending a shot. P2P lending is not available to residents of all states, and some states limit the amount you can invest through any one platform provider. Reasonable consumer protections for a business that is ahead of the government's ability to understand it and create proper regulations. Stick to the larger established companies that possess stronger track records.

While it is simplest to use just one type of investment, there is no rule restricting you from creating a principal bucket that spreads your funds between multiple investments. You could have an MMA for safety, liquidity, and low interest risk combined with a zero-coupon bond to create capital for the participation bucket. You could add to that an intermediate bond fund and a

P2P account for higher blended returns. All that matters is that you are comfortable with your choices. The rationale behind assembling a principal bucket portfolio and how it influences your implementation of the VanderPal Method® is discussed in a later chapter.

First, you have a primer on options before reaching the discussion on the participation bucket. Options are the growth portion or upside provider for the market.

CHAPTER 4

MORE ON OPTIONS

An option is a contract that gives you the right but not the obligation to buy or sell one hundred shares of a stock at a specific price for a predetermined length of time. The contract with the right to buy a stock is a call option, and the contract with the right to sell a stock is a put option. The price at which you may buy or sell is the strike price. The predetermined length of time is set by the expiration date. When you buy an option, the price you pay, the premium, is quoted on a per-share basis and is nonrefundable. The premium is not a credit or partial payment toward the stock.

An AAPL January 19 one hundred call at $5 gives you the right to buy one hundred shares of AAPL at a price of $100 per share anytime between the date you buy the call and January 2019. An AAPL January 19 one hundred put at $5 gives you the right to sell $100 shares of AAPL anytime between the date you buy the put and January 2019. This right costs you a premium of $500 per contract.

When you buy an option, you are known as the *holder*.

When you hold a call, you are speculating that the price of AAPL is going to rise before the expiration date. The strike price is $100, but you paid a $5 premium. Your cost basis is now $105 per share. At any price above $105, you make a profit based on the amount you receive above $105. If the stock goes below $100, the most you can lose is the $500 premium. If the stock closes between $100 and $105, you lose the portion of the premium not covered by the sale of the stock. You sell at $102 and receive $200, but you paid a $500 premium. Your net loss on the trade is $300.

When you hold a put, you are speculating that the price of AAPL is going to fall before the expiration date. Everything works like a call option but in reverse. Your break-even point is now $95. Below $95, you make money. Between $95 and $100, you recover some of your premium. Above $100, the most you can lose is the premium.

When you sell an option, you are known as the *writer*.

The writer receives the premium. The writer of a call option is speculating that the price of AAPL will go down before the expiration date. The writer makes a profit equal to the amount of premium received. If the writer owns the one hundred shares of AAPL, the writer loses out on any profit from a higher price.

You do not have to own the stock to write an option. Selling a call on stock you do not own is known as *writing an uncovered* or *naked call*. You are naked in the sense that any rise in price above the strike plus the premium results in a loss of the entire difference. You are naked in the sense that your loss is theoretically unlimited. If AAPL soars to $300, you lose $195 per share.

Writing the uncovered put works in a similar fashion. You pocket the $500 premium for a $500 profit if the exercised price is above $100. Between $95 and $100, you lose part of the premium. Below $95, you start to lose money, but your long-term loss potential is limited. You can ride all the way down to zero but not below. The most you can lose is $95 per share.

Do not worry; the VanderPal Method® is about lowered risk. You will not be left naked writing uncovered options.

The expiration date of equity options is the Saturday following the third Friday of the month. The closing price of the stock on the third Friday of the month stated on the contract at 4:00 p.m. eastern standard time is used for the determination of an option's value at expiration.

More than four hundred securities now have options that expire on a weekly basis. Weekly options work like regular options, just with shorter time frames. You will not be using short-term options, as the cost over time is significantly higher.

Open interest is a measure of the liquidity of an option. The figure is reported daily and represents the number of outstanding option contracts of a set strike price and expiration date that have been bought or sold to open a position and are currently still open.

If the open interest on a long-term option you're considering is very low, you might want to think twice about making the investment. First, look at shorter-term contracts. If they offer little interest, it is time to check another security. Remember you are a long-term holder. If the short-term liquidity is good, you might still make the investment with a good expectation that liquidity will come to you.

Option volume is the number of contracts that have been bought or sold during the day. Brokers trading platforms report volume numbers on a real-time basis, and charting software can provide the volume numbers for any time frame you choose. Volume is an important measure of liquidity.

The option premium is a combination of the option's intrinsic value and its time value.

The intrinsic value of an option is its value without regard to time. The value of the option at expiration when time has run out is the purest example of intrinsic value. It represents the true value of the option at any point in time. It is the value of the option if you exercised it now. Options almost never trade below their intrinsic value.

The intrinsic value of a call option equals the stock price minus the strike price and can never be less than $0. An option never has a negative value. Like the premium, intrinsic value is stated on a per share basis.

If AAPL is trading at $100 per share, a call option with a strike price of $100 has no intrinsic value as $100 minus $100 equals $0. A call option with a strike price of $95 would have an intrinsic value of $5, and a call option with a strike price of $105 would have an intrinsic value of $0 as it cannot have a value of -$5.

The intrinsic value of a put option equals the strike price less the stock price. If AAPL is trading at $100, a put option with a strike price of $100 has no intrinsic value, a put option with a strike price of $95 has no intrinsic value, and an option with a strike price of $105 has an intrinsic value of $5.

Intrinsic value is also known as the *money*. When the strike price and the stock price of a put or a call are the same, the option is said to be at the money (ATM), and the intrinsic value is zero. When the stock price is greater than the strike price of a call, the call is considered in the money (ITM) as it has intrinsic value. If the stock price is less than the strike price of a call, the call is referred to as being *out of the money (OTM)* and has no intrinsic value.

A put option with a strike price that is more than the stock price is ITM and has intrinsic value. If the strike price of a put is less than the stock price, the put is OTM.

The extrinsic value of an option is known as its *time value*. The time value is equal to the option's premium minus the intrinsic value. The longer an option has to its expiration date, the greater its time value. The time value of a September option will be greater than the time value of a March option. The more time to the expiration date, the greater probability of the stock hitting a profitable price point. The only value out-of-the-money options have is time value. When the expiration date arrives, time value disappears, and the option has only intrinsic value. There are factors that influence time value.

The time value of your option depreciates through a process known as *time decay*. The moment you purchase an option, it begins to lose its time value. An option with a long time to expiration experiences only a small amount of time decay. As the option moves closer and closer to expiration, the rate of time decay accelerates. During the final thirty to sixty days before expiration time, decay occurs rapidly until time value hits zero and only the intrinsic value remains.

Volatility, both historical and implied, influences the calculation of an options time value. Historical volatility is a statistical measurement of the price movements of the underlying security and is usually determined by calculating the standard deviation of the security's daily closing price for the previous month.

Implied volatility is a more esoteric measurement that looks at the direction of stock price movement, the direction of option price movement, the distribution of calls versus puts, and the disparity between the premiums required to purchase puts or calls of the same intrinsic value. All participants in the market, including yourself, are contributors to the calculation of implied volatility.

There are numerous different technical analysis techniques for determining volatility. The fundamental rule is that the flatter a stock's pricing will lower the measurement of volatility and the more erratic a stock's pricing, the higher the volatility. Higher volatility points to a higher risk so that option writers will require compensation in the form of a higher premium. Lower volatility equities and indices can lead to lower cost options on those respective equities or indices.

Exercising Options and Closing Positions

You will want to close your option position at some point during the contract period.

You could exercise the option and take profit. You simply tell your broker that you would like to exercise the option, and your broker, in the case of an ITM call option, will buy the stock from the writer at the strike price and sell the stock at the market price, giving you any intrinsic value above the premium as profit.

If your option is OTM with little time value, you can just let it expire as worthless.

You could rely on the automatic exercise process at the expiration date and receive the intrinsic value above the premium price as profit.

The focus of examples has been on exercising options. One important options factor is that options contracts are tradeable securities contracts. You can choose to offset your option at any point during the contract period.

To offset an option, you simply do the opposite of your original transaction. If you bought a put or call, you simply sell the put or call. The transactions cancel each other out. The difference between your initial premium and the premium you receive in closing out the transaction is your profit or loss.

Why would you want to offset your trade rather than just exercising the option? The answer is time value.

Say you initially purchased an AAPL call with the strike price of $100 for a premium of $5. The stock is now trading at $105, and similar calls are selling for a $6 premium. If you exercise the option, you will receive only the intrinsic value of $5 per share for a total of $500 profit. Sell your call, and you will receive a premium of $6 per share for a total profit of $600.

Most traders choose to offset their options or let them expire worthless on the expiration date and seldom exercise their options. Most options are exercised on the expiration date when the time value has disappeared. There are typically two types of options settlements. American settlement is generally applied to nonindex options such as equity options. European settlement is generally applied in index options.

The Advantages of LEAPS

LEAPS calls provide long-term stock market investors the opportunity to benefit from the growth of large capitalization companies without making large stock purchases.

LEAPS allow holders to take a long-term position of up to three years without needing to worry about short-term expiration dates and rollovers. LEAPS reduce trading costs, and the premiums paid on short-term options exceed the premium paid to buy LEAPS, creating lower monthly costs and higher compounded returns.

Why Use Options

The primary reason for using options is the ability to profit from market movements using leverage while managing risk. The VanderPal Method® uses options to allow you to receive market matching returns while keeping your principal safe.

Encyclopedia-size books exist that cover all the different types and combinations of option strategies. The VanderPal Method® keeps things simple by ignoring all the complicated schemes and primarily buying calls with the rare use of puts in the proper situation.

CHAPTER 5

MORE ON RISK

Now that you have a basic understanding of the principal bucket and options investing, it is time to increase your knowledge of investment techniques to reduce and manage risk. The first step on this journey is an overview of structured products, portfolio insurance, and standard portfolio protection systems.

Structured Products

Structured products are investments that derive their value from an underlying security or group of securities. When you invest in a structured product, you get an interest in the contractual arrangement between the securities but do not have ownership of the underlying securities. The exception is the simplest form of a structured product, a Treasury STRIP.

A Treasury STRIP is a security issued by the US Department of Treasury that acts like one of the more common types of structured securities, zero-coupon bonds. The Treasury STRIP has a face value, but you pay a discounted amount that reflects an interest rate to maturity. You receive no interest payments and are paid the full-face value upon maturity. You own the actual bond.

Zero-coupon bonds, other than STRIPs, are products created by investment banks. While some companies are starting to directly issue debt as zero-coupon bonds, most zero-coupon bonds on corporate bonds and municipal bonds are security contracts underwritten by investment banks using underlying securities they hold as the basis. These securities can be good investments if you pay attention to quality. A zero-coupon from Joe's Corner Investment Bank has little liquidity or safety. A zero-coupon bond from Goldman Sachs is solid, and most of the large investment banks make a market in the securities they issue. Liquidity is one of the selling points that allows them to issue more securities and collect more fees.

The creation of structured products, also known as *derivatives*, is a huge business with total market size estimates between $500 trillion and more than $1.25 quadrillion. By comparison, the total global GDP is slightly more than $77 trillion.

Interest rates, foreign exchange rates, and equity securities are the basis for most derivative products. Most of these contracts are conservative in nature and designed to either protect against market fluctuations or provide slightly higher returns. Equity security structured products can be used for speculation, but the majority are used as portfolio insurance.

Portfolio Insurance

The average investor does not have access to portfolio insurance derivatives that financial institutions, pension funds, and insurance companies use for protection.

The closest you can come to a portfolio protection derivative are investment products from insurance companies that include or offer portfolio protection options. The two most common types of contracts are fixed and variable annuities.

Fixed annuities are insurance policies that bear a similarity to bank CDs as they pay a set interest rate based on the period you commit to keeping your funds in the annuity. The interest rates are generally equal with both products. Both guarantee your principal. The difference is that the CDs are guaranteed by the US government, and the annuity guarantee relies on the financial stability of the insurance company. Insurance companies have rating agencies that grade each company's financial stability on a scale like bond ratings. Only choose products from A-rated companies.

Annuities have an advantage over CDs in that interest payments can accumulate free of taxation. The disadvantage to annuities is that they have surrender charges if you want to remove your money before the end of the guarantee period. An annuity with an eight-year guarantee probably has an 8 percent surrender charge. Banks might reduce your interest rate for early withdrawal, but they return 100 percent of your principal. The surrender charges are the main reason that annuities are not a part of the VanderPal Method®'s principal bucket investment choices.

Variable annuities are a hybrid of securities like mutual funds with insurance features and options. Variable annuities do not pay a set interest rate. You have a range of investment funds to choose from that offer the chance to profit from different types of equity and fixed-income investments. While your returns can be positive or negative, it is possible to insure your principal against loss.

Variable insurance annuity policies have portfolio protection riders available. You pay a premium to protect either the value of your initial investment or the increasing value of your portfolio. The premiums can range between 0.5 percent and 2 percent of your portfolio value on an annual basis with the rate depending upon the features you choose to include. Do not assume that the lowest premium charge is the best. Variable annuities charge fees to cover fund management, expenses, and commissions. Making a valid comparison requires considering all fees, including any surrender charges.

The insurance company can self-insure the risks of portfolio insurance protection by relying on its assets and underwriting experience regarding redemption rates in down markets. The company often has a department dedicated to buying and selling of structured derivatives to mitigate their risk.

While you can receive principal protection within an annuity, the assorted fees are a drag on investment returns. Maybe it is time for you to consider one of the standard methods of portfolio protection.

Portfolio Protection Using Put Options

Put options can be used to speculate on the direction of the market, but they are frequently used to protect portfolios against declines in the market. The put options are an effective risk-management investing strategy that works when the market falls.

Assume that you have $100,000 invested in an S&P 500 Index ETF such as the SPY. The index share value is currently at two hundred, and you are long in the hopes of the economy improving but have some concerns revolving around the Federal Reserve and the political climate. You have gains you do not want to lose but do not want to trigger tax liabilities a stop loss sale would impose. So, you decide to buy one-year put options instead.

The number of ATM put options to buy is determined by dividing your $100,000 by the strike price of $200 and dividing the answer by the one hundred shares in the option. In this case, the answer is five. You must buy five ATM options if the goal is to protect yourself fully from a market meltdown. At a premium of $10, each option will cost $1,000, and your total will be $5,000 or 5 percent of your portfolio value. If the S&P 500 falls 20 percent to

160, your loss is limited to 5 percent paid as the premium. Saving the 15 percent makes the 5 percent premium a good investment.

The problem with using put options for portfolio protection is when the market does not fall. If the market rises 20 percent instead, your gain is limited to 15 percent, and if the gain is 5 percent or less, you lose money. Also, every year you will spend approximately 5 percent of your portfolio to maintain protection.

You could reduce the short-term expense by shortening the expiration period to six months and paying a premium of $3 for a total of $3,000. This is a great strategy if you are worried only about the market falling within the next six months and have no intention of considering portfolio protection after that time. If you do want to keep constant portfolio protection, you have to raise your costs to 5 percent of your portfolio per year.

Given that the current S&P 500 Index annualized five-year return is approximately 14 percent, it makes your annualized fully protected return using the 5 percent strategy only about 9 percent. Over the last fifty years, the S&P 500 Index has increased in thirty-three years and decreased in only seventeen years. The long-term cost of a portfolio protection strategy based on buying put options would have eliminated most to all the profits of investing in the index.

Better Risk Management Investing

There is a much better strategy to use for protecting your portfolio and participating in higher overall market gains while taking less risk. You can use the VanderPal Method® and the market participation bucket.

CHAPTER 6

THE MARKET PARTICIPATION BUCKET

The Vanderpal Method® uses a different system to protect your principal and give you the benefits of long-term market gains. Rather than protect you from losses of principal, the Vanderpal Method® keeps your principal safe and uses a small amount of capital to purchase LEAPS call options to capture market gains.

Why LEAPS Options?

LEAPS options significantly lower the long-term cost of investing in options. An ATM two-year call option on the SPY has a premium of about $20 for a total two-year option cost of $2,000. An ATM one-year call option has a premium of $15 for a one-year option cost of $1,500 and a two-year option cost of $2,000.

The six-month ATM call option has a premium of $9 for a six-month option cost of $900 and totals a two-year option cost of $3,600. Shifting to three-month options has a premium charge of $6 for an option cost over three months of $600. The total cost of using three-month options comes to $4,800 over two years.

The VanderPal Method® is a long-term risk management investment strategy, and lowering costs leads to greater gains over time. You will be profitable at an overall slower rate of growth. The two-year options are less susceptible to the short-term fluctuation of value caused by market noise and the emotional reactions of short-term traders to events in the news cycle.

Using the Participation Bucket

Your principal bucket is securely holding your capital at the appropriate balance of risk versus return for your level of risk tolerance. Now, you take 4 percent of capital and place it in your participation bucket. You use the funds placed in the participation bucket to purchase two-year LEAPS options (SPX) on the S&P 500 Index.

You now have your structured security without having to pay any fees. Going forward, you simply deposit the earnings from your principal account into the participation bucket and buy more LEAPS options. The purchases can be made on an annual, semiannual, or quarterly basis. As time goes by, you establish a stream of steadily expiring LEAPS options that is constantly being replenished. All profits from expiring options transfer to the principal bucket, and all earnings from the principal bucket transfer to the participation bucket.

Full Market Participation Level

The 4 percent initial investment followed by adding in at least 4 percent per year from principal bucket earnings is the input level required for option returns to match stock market returns over time. Why 4 percent? If you have chosen a very conservative place, such as a bank MMA, to hold your principal, you have a decision to make. You can either add capital to investment return and bring it up to 4 percent, or you can move forward with partial participation. It is your decision based on your risk profile. It is important to note that if you are receiving a return on your principal of 4 percent, the annual participation bucket contribution represents a zero-risk investment on your behalf.

The 4 percent figure does not represent full participation in year one of your investing plan. It can take up to two or three full cycles to reach the full participation level of LEAPS option ownership. The cost of options reduces the profits per option in an average year, which requires more options to match the market. In a good year, the leverage options reduce the number of options needed to match the market and can provide market-beating returns.

There are going to be down years in which some of your options can expire with no profit. Remember that over the last fifty years, the S&P 500 Index has had thirty-three up years versus seventeen down years. The trend extends over one hundred years with sixty-seven up years versus thirty-three down years. The one-hundred-year period includes every kind of economic cycle imaginable: world wars, the Great Depression, multiple recessions, high inflation, low inflation, periods of steady growth, investment bubbles, and burst investment bubbles.

Throughout the entire one-hundred-year period, there has been one constant long-term trend, and that is a consistent rise in the value of the S&P 500 Index. There are some lesser trends that are of great value to you as a long-term investor using LEAPS options.

The ratio of up years to down years is two to one, but that does not mean that the market goes up for two years then goes down for one year and repeats the cycle. Most of the down years are a single year inserted into a string of up years. There are a few incidents of two straight down years. However, there are only three occasions in the past one hundred years that the market has been down for three consecutive years.

The first occasion was between 1940 and 1942, a time that marks the early stages of World War II, which was the most disruptive calamity during the entire one hundred years. The second occasion occurred between 2001 and 2003, when the US economy was hit by the double whammy of the dot-com bubble collapse and the terrorist attack on 9/11. The only four-year losing streak took place from 1929 to 1933, which was the first four years of the Great Depression.

Removing those ten years from the equation gives sixty-seven up years versus twenty-three down years. The sixty-seven up years contain several runs of three years or more. The majority of the down years are a single off year in the midst of a longer upper run. Even the 2008 financial crisis meltdown, referred to as the Great Recession, was only a two-year downturn—granted it was major, in the middle of twelve up years.

LEAPS options would have expired without value during those two years. However, the profits achieved during the years before and after that two-year period more than made up for the temporary loss of participation bucket capital. This is made more real by looking at comparisons to two popular investment strategies.

VanderPal Method® versus Passive Index Funds

You are probably wondering what the difference is between the VanderPal Method® and just sticking your money in a passive index fund. A comprehensive study was run using data from January 1995 to December 2004. The ten-year period has some of the most extreme market action of the last one hundred years. The VanderPal Method® of hedging a secure portfolio using LEAPS call options was compared to fully exposed investing in the S&P 500 Index.

Here's a quick recap of market action over the time period. Buoyed by the exploding technology and Internet sector, the S&P 500 had steady and significant gains for five years. The index rose from 465.25 on January 1, 1995, to 1,425.59 on January 1, 2000. Next, the bottom started to fall out of the Internet bubble, and the dot-com bubble was bursting. The market fell steadily, hitting 895.84 on January 1, 2003. The market recovered over the next two years, resting at 1,181.41 on January 1, 2005.

The exposed portfolio managed a geometric annualized return over the ten-year study of 9.97 percent for the VanderPal Method® and 9.72 percent for the S&P 500 Index. An initial $100,000 investment in each would have risen to $258,668 for the VanderPal Method® and $252,847 for the S&P 500 Index—very similar results achieved with much different risk factors as measured by the Sharpe and the Sortino ratios.

The Sharpe ratio tells us whether a portfolio's returns are due to smart investment decisions or a result of excess risk. This measurement is very useful because although one portfolio or fund can reap higher returns than its peers, it is only a good investment if those higher returns do not come with too much additional risk. The greater a portfolio's Sharpe ratio, the better its risk-adjusted performance has been. A negative Sharpe ratio indicates that a riskless asset would perform better than the security being analyzed.

The Sortino ratio was developed by Frank A. Sortino to differentiate between good and bad volatility in the Sharpe ratio. This differentiation of upward and downward volatility allows the calculation to provide a risk-adjusted measure of a security's or fund's performance without penalizing it for upward price changes. The Sortino ratio is like the Sharpe ratio, except it uses downside deviation for the denominator instead of standard deviation, the use of which doesn't discriminate between up and down volatility.

The VanderPal Method® had a Sharpe ratio of 0.3421 and a Sortino ratio of 7.937. The S&P 500 Index had a Sharpe ratio of 0.7980 and a Sortino ratio of 0.5981. The bottom line is that based on the Sortino ratio, the VanderPal Method® has 7.7 percent of the fully exposed S&P 500 Index investment. Stated another way, the S&P 500 Index portfolio was thirteen times more volatile than the VanderPal Method®. The study covered only the one ten-year period, but it is a very fair period in terms of balanced market action.

The Ratcheting Effect

The explanation of the Ratcheting Effect of the participation bucket and how it benefits your principal bucket requires revisiting the S&P 500 Index. Moving forward from the previous study, staying with a January 1 date, options turned a profit in 2006, 2007, and 2008. The options expired without value in 2009 and 2010. Profitability returned for 2011, 2012, 2013, 2014, and 2015. A flattening market caused 2016 to be a year in which the options expired with slightly more than half the premium value remaining as intrinsic value.

The illustration assumes that you invest 4 percent of the $100,000 value of your principal account into the participation account and purchase two-year LEAPS options. The option purchase is in addition to the full $100,000 in the principal bucket earning 4 percent. In each succeeding year, you add the earnings to the participation account and spend the full amount on additional options. In profitable years, any profits more than the premium are placed in the principal account, and the option premiums will roll over into new options. The option premium cost assumes an expectation of an S&P 500 Index increase of 10 percent over the two-year life of the option. The percentage returns on the index are the actual returns of the S&P 500 Index between 2009 and 2017.

You start in 2009 and invest $4,000, purchasing two-year LEAPS options expiring in 2011. In 2010, you invest another $4,000 from earnings to buy two-year LEAPS options expiring in 2012.

You reach 2011, and the S&P 500 Index has risen 48 percent since you bought your options. Subtract the 10 percent figured into the options premium, and you have received the equivalent of a 38 percent increase in the index and the full return of the $4,000 premium. The options provide you with ten-to-one leverage, so your return on the options premium invested is 380 percent. The 380 percent profit on the $4,000 premium is $15,200 that you add to the principal bucket, where it will earn 4 percent. The entire $4,000 premium return is reinvested along with $4,000 from principal-bucket earnings for a total options purchase of $8,000. The new two-year options expire in 2013.

When 2012 comes around, the S&P 500 Index has a two-year rise of 15.8 percent. Allowing for the 10 percent option premium allowance, the increase is 5.8 percent. So, the ten-to-one leverage return on the premiums is 58 percent or $2,320 more for the principal account. The profits from 2011 raised the principal bucket to $115,200. The 4 percent annual return comes to $4,608 for addition to the participation bucket. Taking $4,608 and adding it to the rolling over $4,000 premium, you are buying $8,608 worth of two-year options expiring in 2014.

The two-year increase in the S&P 500 between 2011 and 2013 is 15.4 percent. Adjusting for the premium allowance of 10 percent makes the return 5.4 percent. The leveraged return on your $8,000 premium is 54 percent, which gives you $4,320 to add to the principal bucket. The 2012 profit increased the principal bucket to $117,520, which returned $4,700. You add $4,700 to the rolling over $8,000 premium and purchase $12,700 worth of options expiring in 2015.

Now you are in 2014, and the S&P 500 Index has a two-year increase of 40 percent. After the 10 percent premium adjustment, the return is 30 percent. Factoring the ten-to-one leverage gives you a 300 percent return on the $8,608 premium. You will be adding $25,824 to the principal bucket, raising the total to $147,753. The $8,608 premium is combined with another $4,875 earned in the previous year. You now own $13,783 worth of options expiring in 2016.

The market has another two good years between 2013 and 2015. The S&P 500 Index return is 37 percent. The 10 percent premium allowance gives an index return of 27 percent and a leveraged return of 270 percent on $12,700. This year the principal bucket addition is $34,290. The 2014 earnings on the principal were $5,908. Add $5,908 to the $12,700 of rollover premium and purchase $18,608 worth of two-year options expiring in 2017. The principal bucket's new total combined profits and retained earnings is $181,990.

Between 2014 and 2016, the S&P 500 Index increased by only 5.28 percent, which is not enough to cover the 10 percent premium allotment. You do get 52.8 percent of your $13,483 in premium returned, which equals $7,119. The principal earnings came in at $7,280. You have a total of $14,399 you can put toward new two-year options expiring in 2018.

The period between 2015 and 2017 is not stunning, with an increase of just 12.18 percent. The return is just above the 10 percent premium cost, and you recover all your premium payment of $18,608. This $18,608 plus $7,280 of earnings from principal provides $25,888 to purchase options expiring in 2019. The 21.8 percent leveraged return adds another $4,506 to the principal bucket.

You now see how the ratcheting effect steadily increases the funds going toward LEAPS options premiums and the potential for profits. This example covered only the past eight years. The ratcheting effect gets even stronger as more time passes. You are already purchasing options at a level above that needed for full participation in the returns of the S&P 500 Index.

The straight comparison to the S&P 500 Index for the eight years from 2009 to 2017 shows the S&P 500 Index with a 163 percent gain. A $100,000 account is now worth $263,000.

The VanderPal Method® principal bucket now holds $186,496 for a gain of 86.49 percent. However, that is not the whole story. You still hold $14,399 worth of options expiring in 2018 and $25,888 worth of options expiring in 2019. The S&P 500 Index is up more than 18 percent in 2016, giving you a current profit on your 2018 options of almost $11,509. If you cashed out today, you would have a principal account worth $238,242. The total is still below the S&P 500 Index, but any increase in the index over the next year pushes up the leveraged profit on the 2018 options and contributes to the potential profitability of the 2019 options. A couple of good years, and the VanderPal Method® can overtake the index return.

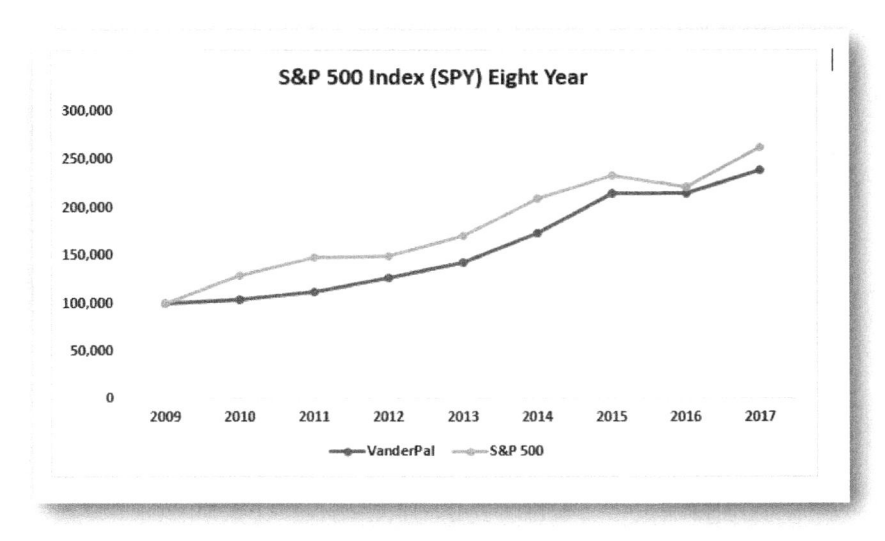

S&P 500 Index (SPY) Eight Year

Of course, markets can go down. So, look at a different ten-year time frame.

Go backward two years and look at the ten years from 2007 to 2017. The same $100,000 initial investment in the S&P 500 Index in 2007 would have fallen 39 percent to $61,000. Between 2009 and 2017, the investment rises 163 percent to $160,387 for a ten-year return of 60.39 percent.

The VanderPal Method®'s primary concern is for the safety of your principal. The $100,000 from 2007 is still worth $100,000 in 2009. The account rises between 2009 and 2017 to having $182,255 in the stable principal bucket and $41,497 worth of options in the participation bucket. The account's cash-out value is $238,242. The ten-year total return is 137.24 percent.

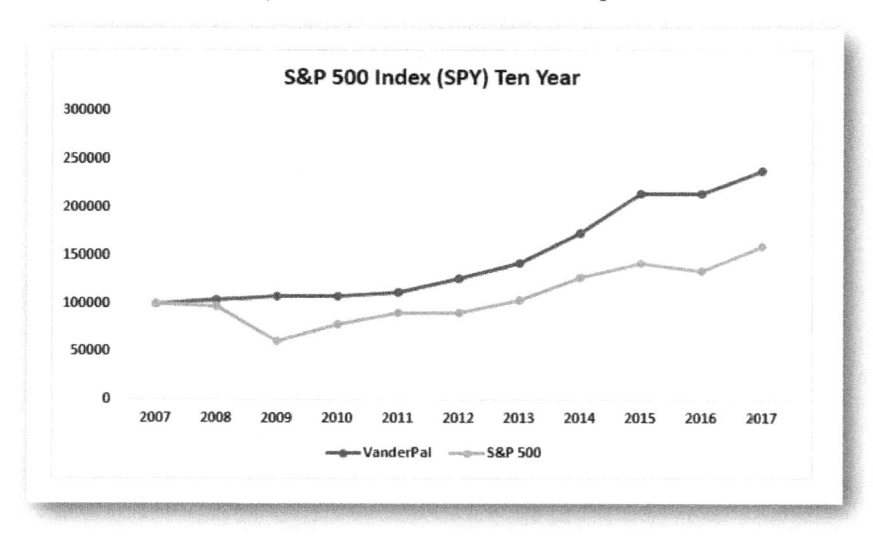

S&P 500 Index (SPY) Ten Year

The ratcheting effect and the stability of principal are further illustrated taking a longer-term view.

The following chart depicts the S&P 500 Index from the beginning of the first VanderPal Method® study to the beginning of

2017. Notice how the avoidance of market downturns combines with the ratcheting effect.

S&P 500 Index 1995 - 2017

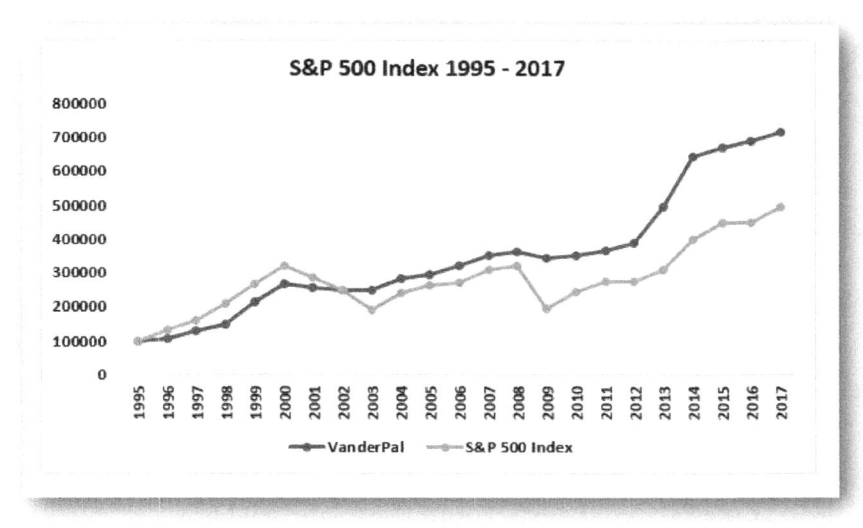

(Chart showing VanderPal vs S&P 500 Index from 1995 to 2017, with values ranging from 0 to 800000)

The values for the VanderPal Method® are the total for the principal and participation buckets. The current value of options going forward is more than $150,000.

Notice the power of the ratcheting effect. Locking in your returns by placing participation profits into the principal bucket sometimes results in lower upside performance compared with a straight vanilla index fund. However, the VanderPal Method® downside risk is near zero, unlike the drops in the fully exposed index fund.

VanderPal Method® versus Variable Annuity

Variable annuities start with a mortality and expense fee that covers the basic underwriting costs of the annuity, a guaranteed death benefit, and future payout options. The exact percentage depends on the exact contract you select, but the industry average is about 1.25 percent. This 1.25 percent is charged against your annuity value every year you own the annuity. There is also an administrative fee to cover the expenses of maintaining your account. The average administrative fee is about 0.25 percent of your account value.

The basic annuity fees already have you up to 1.5 percent with more fees to come.

Investment options, like mutual funds, are called *separate accounts*. You have a wide range of choices covering almost anything that can be managed as an investment, including bonds, stocks, real estate investment trusts, US treasuries, and even some commodities. You can diversify your portfolio by choosing to use multiple accounts. Each separate account has its own fees with a range from 0.5 percent to 3 percent with the average fee being about 1.35 percent. The separate account fees are charged against the value of your account on an annual basis.

There are more fees that can be charged against your account for insurance riders covering things such as long-term health care, increased death benefits, guaranteed minimum income benefits, and principal protection. The only rider that applies to this example is for principal protection.

Principal protection riders can cover the safety of your principal in different manners. Some charge a lower fee in the range of 0.5–1.5 percent per year to guarantee the initial value of your principal for a set number of years, which frequently matches the number of years that the surrender charge on the annuity lasts and protection ends after the set time frame. Other riders will cover both the initial principal and any gains in portfolio value at an average additional expense of 1.75 percent and provide that coverage for as long as you own the annuity.

Adding up the average mortality and expense fee, administrative fee, the separate account fees, and principal protection fees bring you to a total of 4.5 percent. The 4.5 percent is charged against your account value every year until you give up the annuity.

The 4.5 percent paid in fees ensures that you will never match market performance. In the current interest rate environment, the fees exceed the returns available from any of the fixed-income-based separate accounts.

In the interest of fairness to the variable annuity industry, it should be noted that if you shop around, you can find a highly rated variable annuity account that provides all services described above for a total fee of 2 percent. You still will pay the fee based on your entire account value.

The VanderPal Method® has discount commission charges on LEAPS options purchases. If you are using a mutual fund or ETF as part of your principal bucket, there will be a small expense fee. There are no other fees.

A variable annuity does have one advantage over the standard VanderPal Method® account. The earnings within the annuity are not taxed as they are earned. You pay taxes only when you start to take money out of the account.

The VanderPal Method® account does not need to be taxable. There is nothing that stops you from setting up your VanderPal Method® account within an existing IRA account or in a 401k account that allows self-directed trading. If you are lucky enough to have a Roth retirement plan to use, you can avoid all taxes on accumulating earnings and withdrawals.

Variable annuity accounts can offer a rider for a guaranteed income, which is not available with a VanderPal Method® account. Of course, there will be a fee for the rider that you will pay on your entire principal balance every year.

The reason to keep bringing variable annuities into the conversation is they are the closest form of structured securities product available to noninstitutional investors that have the potential for principal security provided by the VanderPal Method®.

The biggest difference is that a variable annuity always has the drag of the fees on investment returns, and when investment returns do not exceed the fees, principal is reduced. The VanderPal Method® account never has a fee against principal or a drag on the earnings of the principal bucket except for low-cost ETF fees or fees to purchase certain securities.

Yes, a case could be made that in a year when LEAPS options expire with no value, the loss of premium is similar to the fee lost to the variable annuity underwriter. However, in a profitable year for the principal bucket, you get all the capital back with the VanderPal Method® when a variable annuity holder would still be paying the full fees, and keep in mind the dividends or interest generated from the principal bucket offset the option premiums.

An interesting way to view the comparison is on the basis of annuity fees versus principal bucket LEAPS options premiums. It's a simple matter of comparing the rates of return.

Your 2–4.5 percent fee to the annuity underwriter is a no-risk investment. You are guaranteed to lose the money, and there is absolutely no way to ever profit off those funds. Once you pay the fee, the money is gone for good. The rate of return on the fees is 0 percent.

Using the VanderPal Method®, the money you are not paying in fees, as well as option returns, gets placed into the principal participation bucket for increased interest or dividend earnings for the purchase of LEAPS options. The worst case is that the options expire with no value and you have the same 0 percent return you have with the annuity contract.

However, the best case is that the LEAPS options expire with increased intrinsic value, and you have profits ranging from 1 percent to 500 percent on that capital. These are real profits to add to your principal bucket that will earn additional income to use for the purchase of more LEAPS options in the future.

It is a simple comparison between an absolute guaranteed loss and the potential for gains that expand and accelerate profitability. You can have a guaranteed 2–4.5 percent loss or a possibility of increasing your compounded returns.

Going back to the S&P 500 examples, you can do a numbers comparison between the VanderPal Method® and variable annuity returns.

In the 1995–2004 study, the VanderPal Method® had a geometric annualized return of 9.97 percent versus 9.72 percent for the S&P 500 Index. Assume that you have your funds in a separate account that invests in equity securities and matches the return of the S&P 500 Index. Make another assumption that you have a top-rated variable annuity that charges the lowest expense fee of 2 percent.

The 2 percent annual expense fee reduces your annualized return to 7.72 percent. An initial $100,000 investment in the annuity increases to $210,360 compared to $258,266 for the VanderPal Method®. If your annuity was charging the average fee of 4.75 percent, your account would be worth only $162,424. Stretching to a twenty-year time frame, the VanderPal Method® account is worth $669,089. The 2 percent fee annuity has a value of $442,513, and the 4.75 percent fee annuity is worth only $263,817.

Looking at the eight-year period from 2009 to 2017, the S&P 500 Index's annualized return is 12.3 percent, and the VanderPal Method®'s rate of return is 10.59 percent. The 2 percent fee drops the annuity's annualized return to 10.3 percent. The 4.75 percent fee annuity has annualized returns of 7.55 percent.

The bottom line observation is that the VanderPal Method® returns exceed those of the variable annuity even in the most favorable of circumstances. The annuity fees are a drag on returns in both the short-term and the long-term periods. The longer the time frame, the more dramatic the difference becomes.

A secondary lesson is that if you must buy an annuity, shop for the lowest-possible fees. Keep in mind the ratchet effect of the VanderPal Method® does not exist for a variable annuity.

Addressing the guaranteed income option with annuities, remember that the insurance companies will always be willing to sell you an immediate annuity with a guaranteed for-life payment. Using the VanderPal Method® to accumulate profits gives you a bigger pool of money from which to receive income or the possibility of setting up a guaranteed income and keeping additional funds in the VanderPal Method® account to generate profit to help beat inflation.

The next chapter covers alternative investments for use with the VanderPal Method® and some different strategies.

CHAPTER 7

Alternate Investment Choices

All the previous examples illustrated the investing of participation bucket funds into LEAPS options based on the S&P 500 Index options as represented by SPY. There are two other broad market-based ETFs that offer LEAPS options and a different type of market exposure.

NASDAQ 100 Index (QQQ)

The PowerShares QQQ Trust Series 1 (QQQ) is an ETF that tracks the NASDAQ 100 index. The NASDAQ 100 index includes the most actively traded one hundred companies listed on the NASDAQ. The index includes companies in the retail, industrial, biotechnology, health care, technology, and other sectors. The one sector exception is that there are no financial companies included in the NASDAQ 100 index.

The NASDAQ 100 index provides participation in the more dynamic higher-growth sectors of the US economy. The index's volatility is greater than that of the S&P 500 Index, and the returns are higher in most uptrends. LEAPS option cost risk is only a small amount higher in downtrends.

The NASDAQ 100 index has a very heavy concentration in the technology sector with almost 60 percent of assets invested in technology stocks. The technology emphasis is a positive to some investors and a negative to others.

Additionally, the index is heavily weighted to a few large capitalization stocks. Apple Inc. alone represents 10.9 percent of the net asset value of the index, followed by two classes of Alphabet Inc. (Google) stock at a combined 9.06 percent. The top ten portfolio holdings are rounded out by Microsoft (8.33 percent), Amazon.com Inc. (6.61 percent), Facebook (5.41 percent), Comcast Corp. (2.97 percent), Intel Corp. (2.97 percent), Cisco Systems Inc. (2.59 percent), and Amgen Inc. (1.97 percent). The top ten holdings comprise 47.84 percent of the portfolio. The remaining ninety companies make up the rest of the portfolio.

Before you decide to choose to invest using the NASDAQ 100 index, take a good look at the top ten holdings and ask yourself if you believe in the future of those ten companies. In fairness, you should contrast the NASDAQ 100 with the S&P 500.

The S&P 500 Index is broadly based across all economic sectors. The top ten portfolio holdings are Apple Inc. (3.13 percent), Microsoft Corp. (2.39 percent), Berkshire Hathaway (1.91 percent), Amazon.com Inc. (1.9 percent), Exxon Mobil Corporation (1.72 percent), Johnson & Johnson (1.51 percent), Facebook Inc. (1.47 percent), JPMorgan Chase & Co. (1.46 percent), Alphabet Inc. (1.38 percent), and Wells Fargo & Company (1.33 percent). A second class of Alphabet shares brings the total fund concentration of Alphabet stock to approximately 2.75 percent. The total percentage of S&P 500 Index concentration in the top ten holdings is 19.57 percent versus the 47.84 percent for the NASDAQ 100. Ask yourself which set of companies you believe will have the best performance over the next two years.

The top ten holding for either index is fluid as both the S&P 500 Index and the NASDAQ 100 index rebalance on a quarterly basis. Individual components move around per their individual performances in relation to the overall market. Both the SPY and the QQQ provide current holdings on the funds' detail pages on the underwriters' websites.

A factor to consider is how the NASDAQ 100's performance compares to that of the S&P 500 for a recent period. The easiest comparison is to use the 2009–2017 market run.

You start in 2009 and invest $4,000 in two-year QQQ LEAPS options expiring in 2011. In 2010, you invest another $4,000 from earnings to buy two-year QQQ LEAPS options expiring in 2012.

You reach 2011, and the NASDAQ 100 index has risen 83 percent since you bought your options. Subtract the 10 percent figured into the options premium, and you have received the equivalent of a 73 percent increase in the index and the full return of the $4,000 premium. The options provide you with ten-to-one leverage, so your return on the options premium invested is 730 percent. The 730 percent profit on the $4,000 premium is $29,200 that you add to the principal bucket, where it will earn 4 percent. The entire $4,000 premium return is reinvested along with $4,000 from principal bucket earnings for a total options purchase of $8,000. The new two-year options expire in 2013.

When 2012 comes around, the NASDAQ 100 index has a two-year rise of 22.44 percent. Allowing for the 10 percent option premium allowance, the increase is 12.44 percent. So, the ten-to-one leverage return on the premiums is 124.4

percent or $4,976 more for the principal account. The profits from 2011 raised the principal bucket to $129,200. The 4 percent annual return comes to $5,168 for addition to the principal bucket. Adding $5,168 to the rolling over $4,000 premium, you are buying $9,168 worth of two-year options expiring in 2014.

The two-year increase in the NASDAQ 100 between 2011 and 2013 is 19.97 percent. Adjusting for the premium allowance of 10 percent makes the return 9.97 percent. The leveraged return on your $8,000 of premium is 99.7 percent, which gives you $7,976 to add to the principal bucket. The 2012 profit increased the principal bucket to $134,176, which returned $5,367. You add $5,367 to the rolling over $8,000 premium and purchase $13,536 worth of options expiring in 2015.

Now you are in 2014, and the NASDAQ 100 index has a two-year increase of 57.69 percent. After the 10 percent premium adjustment, the return is 47.69 percent. Factoring the ten-to-one leverage gives you a 476.9 percent return on the $9,168 premium. You will be adding $43,722 to the principal bucket, raising the total to $185,874. The $9,168 premium combines with the $5,686 earned by the principal bucket in the previous year. You now own $14,854 worth of options expiring in 2016.

The market has another two good years between 2013 and 2015. The NASDAQ 100 index return is 59.2 percent. The 10 percent premium allowance gives an index return of 49.2 percent and a leveraged return of 492 percent on $13,536. This year, the principal bucket addition is $66,597. The 2014 earnings on the principal were $7,435. Add $7,435 to the rolling over $13,536 premium and purchase $20,971 worth of two-year options expiring in 2017. The principal bucket's new total combined profits and retained earnings is $252,471.

Between 2014 and 2016, the NASDAQ 100 index increased by 27.88 percent, which, after subtracting the 10 percent premium allotment, comes to 17.88 percent. You get a 178.8 percent return on your $14,854 premium, which equals $26,558. The principal earnings came in at $10,099. You have a total of $24,683 you can put toward new two-year options expiring in 2018. The principal has risen to $279,029.

The period between 2015 and 2017 is not stunning, with an increase of just 14.78 percent. Your leveraged return on the $20,971 worth of options is 47.8 percent or $10,024. Rolling over the recovered option premium $20,971 plus $11,161 of earnings from principal provides $32,132 to purchase options expiring in 2019.

Once again, you see how the ratcheting effect steadily increases the funds going toward LEAPS options premiums and the potential for profits. This example covered only the past eight years. The ratcheting effect gets even stronger as more time passes. You are already purchasing options at a level above that needed for full participation in the returns of the NASDAQ 100 index.

The straight comparison to the NASDAQ 100 index for the eight years from 2009 to 2017 show the NASDAQ 100 index with a 301 percent gain. A $100,000 account is now worth $401,000.

The VanderPal Method®'s principal bucket now holds $289,053 for a gain of 189 percent. However, that is not the whole story. You still hold $24,683 worth of options expiring in 2018 and $32,136 worth of options expiring in 2019. The NASDAQ 100 index rose 5.89 percent in 2016, giving you a current profit on your 2018 options of $1,454. If you cashed out today, you would have a principal account worth $347,326. The total is still below the NASDAQ 100 index, but any increase in the index over the next year pushes up the leveraged profit on the 2018 options and contributes to the potential profitability of the 2019 options. A couple of good years, and the VanderPal Method® can overtake the index return.

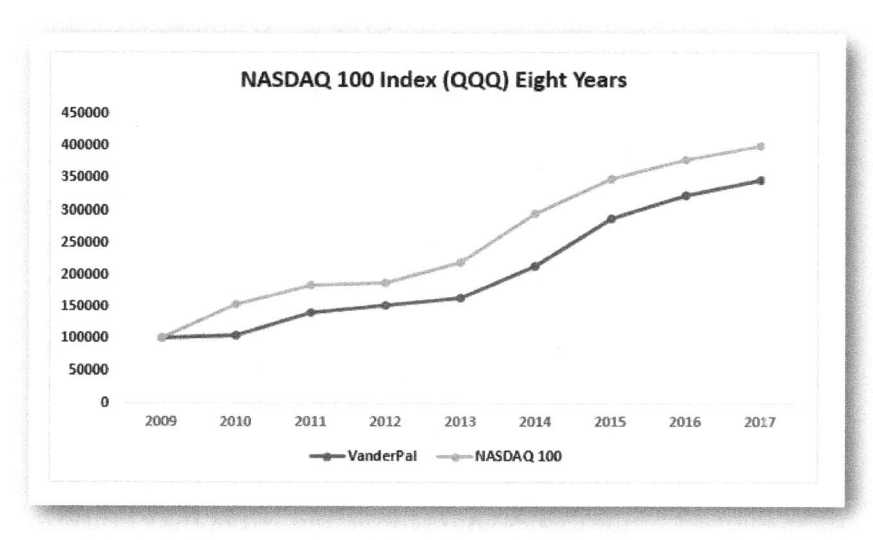

NASDAQ 100 Index (QQQ) Eight Years

Of course, markets can go down. So, look at a different ten-year time frame.

Go backward two years and look at the ten years from 2007 to 2017. The same $100,000 initial investment in the NASDAQ 100 index in 2007 would have fallen 31 percent to $69,000. Between 2009 and 2017, the investment rises 301 percent to $276,690 for a ten-year return of 176.69 percent.

The VanderPal Method®'s primary concern is for the safety of your principal. The $100,000 from 2007 is still worth $100,000 in 2009. The account rises between 2009 and 2017 to having $289,053 in the stable principal bucket and $58,273 worth of options in the participation bucket. The account's cash-out value is $347,326. The ten-year total return is 247.33 percent.

NASDAQ 100 Index (QQQ) Ten Years

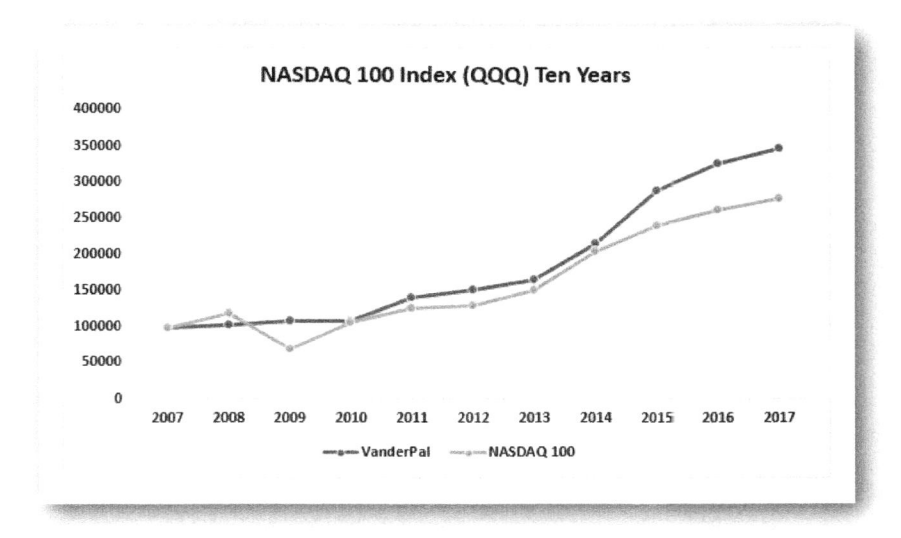

The following chart depicts the S&P 500 Index from the beginning of the first VanderPal Method® study to the beginning of 2017. Notice how the avoidance of market downturns combines with the ratcheting effect.

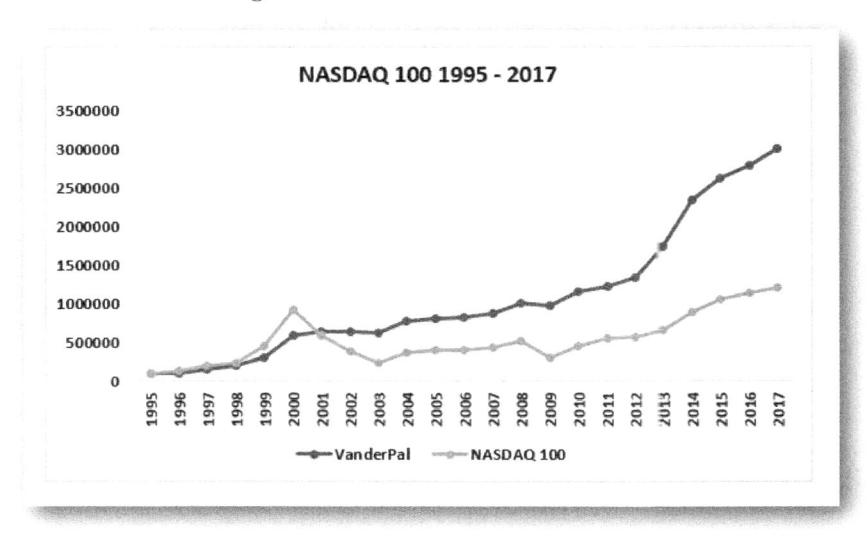

NASDAQ 100 1995 - 2017

67

The values for the VanderPal Method® are the total for the principal and participation buckets. The current value of options going forward is more than $475,000.

Dow Industrial Average (DIA)

The SPDR Dow Jones Industrial Average ETF Trust (DIA) is another possibility for LEAPS options investing. The DIA tracks the Dow Jones Industrial Average (DJIA). The Dow Jones Industrial Average, also called the DOW, is composed of thirty of the most significant large US companies traded on the NASDAQ and NYSE.

The DOW attempts to include companies from a range of sectors that will cover the broad range of overall economic activity. Only one company, General Electric (GE), has been in the index since its inception in 1928. The five largest components of the DJIA are Goldman Sachs Group Inc. (8.04 percent), 3M Company (6.05 percent), International Business Machines Corporation (6.05 percent), Boeing Company (5.52 percent), and UnitedHealth Group Incorporated (5.52 percent). A full list of all DOW component stocks is available from State Street Global Advisors product page for the DIA.

Being composed of large, established companies gives the DJIA a stodgier historic performance that is more stable over the long term.

You start in 2009 and invest $4,000 in purchasing two-year DIA LEAPS options expiring in 2011. In 2010, you invest another $4,000 from earnings to buy two-year LEAPS options expiring in 2012.

You reach 2011, and the DJIA has risen 32 percent since you bought your options. Subtract the 8 percent figured into the options premium, and you have received the equivalent of a 24 percent increase in the index and the full return of the $4,000 premium. The options provide you with ten-to-one leverage, so your return on the options premium invested is 240 percent. The 240 percent profit on the $4,000 premium is $9,600 that you add to the principal bucket, where it will earn 4 percent. The entire $4,000 premium return reinvests along with $4,000 from principal bucket earnings for a total options purchase of $8,000. The new two-year options expire in 2013.

When 2012 comes around, the DOW has a two-year rise of 17.2 percent. Allowing for the 8 percent option premium allowance, the increase is 9.2 percent. So, the ten-to-one leverage return on the premiums is 92 percent or $3,680 more for the principal account. The profits from 2011 raised the principal bucket to $109,600. The 4 percent annual return comes to $4,384 to add to the participation bucket. You are buying $8,384 worth of two-year options expiring in 2014.

The two-year increase in the DJIA between 2011 and 2013 is 13.2 percent. Adjusting for the premium allowance of 8 percent makes the return 5.2 percent. The leveraged return on your $8,000 premium is 52 percent, which gives you $4,168 to add to the principal bucket. The 2012 profit increased the principal bucket to $113,280, which returned $4,531. You add $4,531 to the $8,000 premium rolling over and purchase $12,531 worth of options expiring in 2015.

Now you are in 2014, and the DOW index has a two-year increase of 35.7 percent. After the 8 percent premium adjustment, the return is 27.7 percent. Factoring the ten-to-one leverage gives you a 277 percent return on the $8,384 premium. You will be adding $23,224 to the principal bucket, raising the total to $140,664. The $8,384 premium combines with the $4,698 earned in the previous year. You now own $13,082 worth of options expiring in 2016.

The market has another two good years between 2013 and 2015. The DJIA return is 36 percent. The 8 percent premium allowance gives an index return of 28 percent and a leveraged return of 280 percent on $12,531. This year, the principal bucket addition is $35,086. The 2014 earnings on the principal were $5,627. Add $5,627 to the $12,531 of rollover premium and purchase $18,158 worth of two-year options expiring in 2017. The principal bucket's new total combined profits and retained earnings is $175,750.

Between 2014 and 2016, the DOW increased by only 5.1 percent, which is not enough to cover the 8 percent premium allotment. You do get 51 percent of your $13,082 in premium returned, which equals $6,672. The principal earnings came in at $7,030. You have a total of $13,702 you can put toward new two-year options expiring in 2018.

The period between 2015 and 2017 is not stunning, with an increase of just 10.9 percent. It's slightly above the 8 percent premium cost, but you get a 29 percent leveraged return on your premium payment of $18,158 and put $5,266 into the principal bucket, which now contains $187,688. The premium rollover plus $7,030 of earnings from principal provides $25,188 to purchase options expiring in 2019.

You once more see how the ratcheting effect steadily increases the funds going toward LEAPS options premiums and the potential for profits. This example covered only the past eight years. The ratcheting effect gets even stronger as more time passes. You are already purchasing options at a level above that needed for full participation in the returns of the Dow Jones Industrial Index.

A straight comparison to the DOW index for the eight years from 2009 to 2017 show the DJIA with a 125 percent gain. A $100,000 account is now worth $225,000.

The VanderPal Method®'s principal bucket now holds $181,016 for a gain of 81 percent. However, that is not the whole story. You still hold $13,702 worth of options expiring in 2018 and $25,188 worth of options expiring in 2019. The DOW index is up 13.42 percent in 2016, giving you a current profit on your 2018 options of $7,426. If you cashed out today, you would have a principal account worth $227,442. The total is slightly above the DOW index, but any increase in the index over the next year pushes up the leveraged profit on the 2018 options and contributes to the potential profitability of the 2019 options. A couple of good years and the VanderPal Method® significantly exceeds the index return.

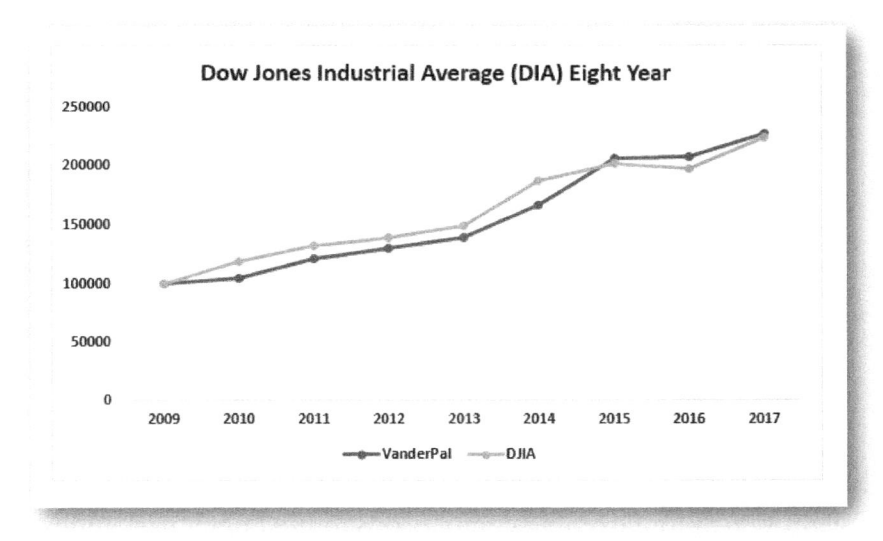

Dow Jones Industrial Average (DIA) Eight Year

Of course, markets can go down. So, look at a different ten-year time frame.

Go backward two years and look at the ten years from 2007 to 2017. The same $100,000 initial investment in the DJIA in 2007 would have fallen 29.6 percent to $70,400. Between 2009 and 2017, the investment rises 125 percent to $158,400 for a ten-year return of 58 percent.

The VanderPal Method®'s primary concern is for the safety of your principal. The $100,000 from 2007 is still worth $100,000 in 2009. The account rises between 2009 and 2017 to having $181,016 in the stable principal bucket and $46,426 worth of options in the participation bucket. The account's cash-out value is $227,442. The ten-year total return is 127.44 percent.

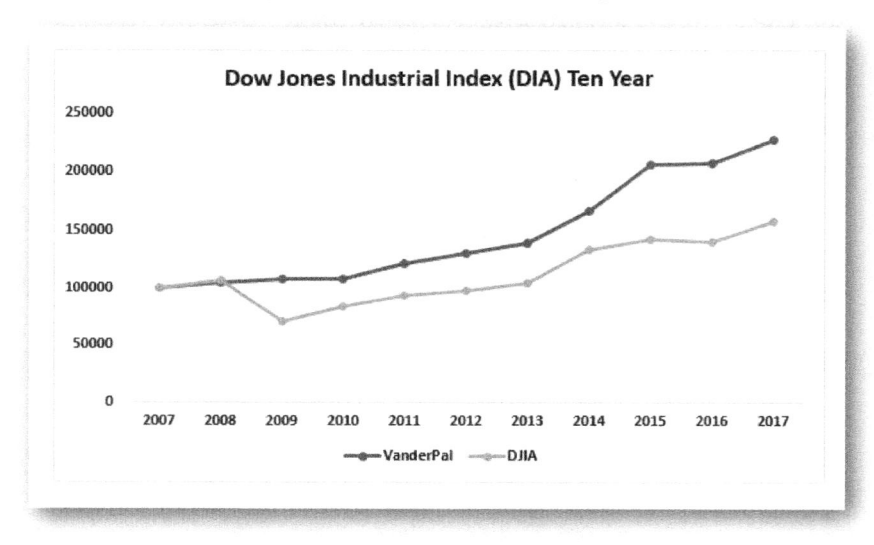

Dow Jones Industrial Index (DIA) Ten Year

You now have three different choices of LEAPS options based on index-driven ETFs to use with the VanderPal Method®. All LEAPS option strategies have given solid returns over the last eight years with favorable comparisons to the benchmark indexes while assuming a much lower level of risk. The ten-year period shows all three VanderPal LEAPS option investments significantly outperforming their corresponding benchmark indexes.

Options for Larger Accounts

If you have a larger account, you do not need to invest in ETF LEAPS options based on the indexes. Instead, you can purchase LEAPS options based directly on the individual indexes themselves.

The S&P 500 Index Options (SPX) from the Chicago Board Options Exchange are a very popular investment tool for institutional investors. The SPX has high volume, high open interest, and LEAPS options. The problem for many investors is the difference in capital required compared with the SPY ETF options.

The value of an investment covered by the SPY is ten times the current value of the index. If the S&P 500 Index is two thousand, a single option's investment value is $20,000. The LEAPS option premium is approximately $2,000.

The value of an investment covered by the SPX is one hundred times the current value of the index. If the S&P 500 Index is two thousand, a single option's investment value is $200,000. The LEAPS option premium is approximately $20,000.

Account suitability for using SPY options starts at $50,000. Account suitability for the SPX options starts at $500,000. There is very little investment return variation between the SPY and the SPX. The only differences for larger accounts are the slightly lower commission fees based on the number of contracts required and the slightly tighter spreads on the SPX. The SPY has a miniscule pricing variation to allow for the small expense fee charged by the underlying ETF.

An S&P mini-option (XSP) is available. Like the SPY, the XSP option represents one-tenth the value of the full S&P index. However, traders prefer the SPY ETF, and the XSP has extremely low trading volume and open interest. There are currently no LEAPS options available.

If the NASDAQ 100 is your investment choice, the NASDAQ 100 Index options (NDX) are available. The NDX uses a value multiplier of $100 times the index. The current contract value is in excess of $500,000 with a single LEAPS option premium of more than $50,000. Account suitability for NDX utilization is $1 million.

There has been an attempt to create a mini-option of the MDX with one-tenth the value of the NDX. Trading volume and open interest are so low as to negate the usefulness of the MDX as an investment.

The primary NASDAQ 100 index investment vehicle is the highly popular QQQ, as it represents a value equal to one-fortieth of the NASDAQ 100 index. The lower barrier to entry makes the QQQ suitable for accounts of $25,000 or more.

The Dow Jones Industrial Average's direct index option is the DJX. Unlike the SPX and the NDX, the DJX does not represent the full value of the benchmark index. The DJX has a value equal to one-hundredth of the DJA—the same level of valuation as the DIA ETF. The result is that the DJX options and the DIA options are interchangeable as investment vehicles.

The DIA does have slightly higher volume and open interest, but the DJX has a sufficient level of volume and open interest to serve as a trading choice. There can be a difference in tax treatment between the DIA and the DJX. We will address taxes in a later section.

There is one more stock market index available to large accounts, the Russell 2000 Index (RUT). The Russell 2000 Index measures the performance of the smallest two thousand companies from a list of the three thousand largest stocks in the United States. The index includes only common stocks of US corporations traded on the NASDAQ, NYSE, or AMEX. The Russell 2000 Index is capitalization weighted and adjusted each June to reflect changes in rankings and shares outstanding.

The RUT provides interesting exposure to small-cap companies. The valuation on the whole group of two thousand stocks tends toward greater stability than the larger-cap, less-diversified indexes and often has greater returns in strong up markets.

The RUT has a valuation of one hundred times the Russell 2000 Index. The large notional size of RUT contracts restricts its suitability to accounts with more than $350,000 in the principal bucket.

There is a large ETF that tracks the Russell 2000 Index. The iShares Russell 2000 ETF (IWM) does offer options, but there is no activity in the two-year or greater options. Depending on the time of year, the best you can invest in are options that expire in one to one and a half years. You can choose to use IWM options in your account if you are willing to have greater options expense over time.

Smaller Accounts

If your account is not yet large enough to purchase index-based ETF options, you can choose to start by investing in LEAPS options based on individual stocks. While most larger companies have options available, not all companies have LEAPS options. Many of the options do not trade with acceptable levels of volume or open interest.

The main criteria for choosing an individual stock is that it must have a beta of less than one. Beta is a measure of the volatility of the stock in relation to a broader benchmark index such as the S&P 500 Index. If a stock's beta is greater than one, its price is more volatile than the index. If a stock's beta is less than one, it has lower volatility than the index. Beta measures the theoretical systemic risk of a security over a unit of time. When checking a stock's volatility, make sure you know the time period used for the beta calculation provided. Many stock quotation sites use only a ninety-day period, which provides a simple measure of short-term volatility. Many stocks with a ninety-day beta of less than one have a long-term history of outperforming the general market.

Picking stocks for use with the VanderPal Method® requires only light analysis. Make a list of large companies that you like, companies that you think have good prospects over the next couple of years or more. Do a quick Internet search for news stories about the companies just to make sure there is no negative information about the companies' prospects of which you are unaware.

Next, take each company from your list and find its ticker symbol. Do a search for the ticker symbol's option chain. A stock's option chain provides a full list of available options and trading information. A search for "GE options chain" provides a list of sites that display the full GE option chain. If you already have a brokerage account, the broker's free software and data services should provide you with detailed options chains and more.

Look at the option chain to see if there is a LEAPS option trading one to two and a half years out that has some open interest and trading volume. Check the options available thirty, sixty, and ninety days out to see if they have active trading volume and open interest. Determine the premium per option and add it to a condensed list of companies that you are seriously considering using for your participation bucket portfolio.

Finally, determine your participation bucket budget and select the company or companies you want to invest in and do it. Buy only one option in each company and use additional funds to invest in other companies. If your budget allows investing in multiple companies, spread the investments across companies in different market sectors.

What you end up with is an options portfolio of conservative defensive stocks that serve as a capital builder for you to reach the point of using index-based ETF LEAPS options. The individual stock options are also a method for investing any extra money left over after buying the maximum number of index-based options your budget can cover.

Using index-based options is the simplest way to manage participation account assets. However, you can expand beyond the easy set it up and do not worry about it plan and use individual stock based options if it works for your investment style.

You do want to pay ongoing attention to any news that could have a long-term negative impact on the individual company. Such an event might be a sign to cash out your options and invest in a different company.

Greater Leverage

There is one more possible alternative options investment. The Direxion Daily S&P 500 Bull 3X Shares ETF (SPXL) is an ETF that attempts to provide a daily investment return of 300 percent of the return of the S&P 500. Put another way, the fund strives to achieve a short-term beta of three. If the S&P 500 Index rises by 1 percent, the fund should rise by 3 percent.

The SPXL design is for short-term trading by people looking to profit off daily volatility—hence the word *daily* in the fund's name. Direxion clearly states that investors should not expect 300 percent of the benchmark's cumulative return over periods greater than one day.

Now that you know the disclaimer, look at the longer-term returns. Over the past five years, the S&P 500 has an annualized total return of 13.71 percent. The Direxion Bull 3X has an annualized total return of 35.7 percent. The one-year return for the S&P 500 Index is 22.77 percent, while the SPXL returned 72.64 percent for the past year. It's not 300 percent but close enough for horseshoes. Over the past ten years, the S&P 500 Index has a total cumulative return of approximately 150 percent compared to almost 600 percent for the SPXL.

Before you get too greedy, remember that what goes up must come down. If the market drops 10 percent, an investment in the

SXPL will lose around 30 percent of its value. Fortunately, there are options for managing risk.

The SPXL does not have full two-year LEAPS options. Depending on the date, the best you can get is nine to fifteen months—not the ideal time frame, but the SXPL options can provide greater market participation with no more risk than the options premium.

The SPXL options are a viable choice if you want to be very conservative with your principal bucket funds but wish to enjoy full participation. Taking 1.5 percent interest from an insured limited-term CD and investing only the interest in the participation bucket, the 1.5 percent of capital invested in SPXL calls should yield the same return over time as 4 percent invested in SPY calls.

Investment examples have shown that 4 percent of capital invested and reinvested in LEAPS options tend to match or exceed the return of the market indexes over ten-year time frames. This is the amount of capital needed to hit a full participation level eventually. Use of SPXL call options can get you to the full participation level sooner.

Your participation bucket budget calls for purchasing two SPY LEAPS options. Instead, you buy one SPY option and one SPXL option. You have the participation equivalent of four SPY options and are close to the full participation point at the start. You might also choose to add a little extra capital and buy two SPY options and one SPXL option. You are slightly above the full participation point with the equivalent of five SPY options. If the numbers are run through the previous SPY investment examples, the investment return using the VanderPal Method® is doubled.

Another example of a good use for the SPXL is for younger investors with small retirement accounts who want to develop a portfolio that will yield returns significantly superior to benchmark market returns over a long time frame.

You have changed jobs and have a small 401k account from your old employer that you are rolling over into an IRA account. You plan to use your new employer's 401k plan to accumulate more retirement funds in the standard selection of mutual funds. You are willing to take a slightly greater risk with your new self-directed rollover IRA.

You invest most of the IRA funds into a medium-term bond ETF that yields close to 4 percent. You use some of your capital to buy at least one SPXL option. If the account is small, the option premium might be larger than 4 percent of capital, but you are young, and this is a good time to take higher risks. If the premium is less than 10 percent of your capital, buy more options. Now just work the system for the next twenty, thirty, or forty years.

CHAPTER 8

SELECTING THE PROFITABLE OPTIONS

There are dozens of strategies for selecting the most profitable options, most of which involve analyzing the "Greeks." The Greeks are formulations using past information that provides possible information about future volatility, pricing, and return.

The first Greek is delta, which is the measurement of change in the options value versus the underlying asset price. A delta ranges from zero to one, and the higher the delta, the higher the relationship of price movement. An option with a delta of 0.8 moves eighty cents when the underlying asset moves $1 in value. Options with higher Deltas are more expensive than low delta options, when ITM and closer to expiration. Gamma is many times used in conjunction with delta, which provides how fast an option's Delta responds to underlying price movements expressed as a percentage. Options with high gammas have highly responsive deltas.

The next Greek is theta, which relates to time decay and sensitivity. All options lose value over time as the option moves closer to expiration. Theta is not constant, and time decay can have different effects based upon whether the option is in, at, or out of the money. Options with low theta values decay slower and have more time to expire than higher theta measurements.

An additional measurement is vega, which relates to measuring rates of volatility changes. Two types of volatility exist: historical and implied. Historical volatility is a measurement of price movements over time, providing a sort of standard deviation proxy. Implied volatility, used in many options pricing models, is a measure of pricing affected by supply and demand for the option.

The last major Greek measurement is rho, which provides a measurement of the option value based on interest rate movements. Because interest rates change slowly over time, this measurement is used more for longer-term options such as LEAPS.

Your eyes are probably glazing over at the thought of making sense of how to use the Greeks. You probably do not even want to hear about Black-Scholes calculations or any of the heavy mathematical theories.

Good news! You can avoid all the heavy calculations and simply use the VanderPal Ratio.

The VanderPal Ratio assumes that all the big traders have done all the heavy mathematical lifting and that all the calculations are already built into the bid and ask prices for options premiums. All you need to do is find the option with the lowest cost per unit of time.

Calculating the VanderPal Ratio is easy. You take the options premium and divide it by the number of months (weeks) left until the expiration date. The result is the VanderPal Ratio, which equals the average monthly (weekly) premium cost of the option. The VanderPal Method® assumes that the most profitable option to invest in is the option with the lowest ratio cost and that remains ATM.

An ATM SPY call expiring in three months has a premium of $540. This amount divided by three yields a monthly cost of $180. An ATM SPY option expiring in twelve months has a premium of $1,200. This amount divided by twelve equals $100. An ATM SPY option expiring in twenty-four months has a premium of $2,100. This amount divided by twenty-four equals $87.50.

In this example, the lowest VanderPal Ratio belongs to the SPY option that expires in twenty-four months, and it is the option with the most profit potential. Most of the time, the lowest VanderPal Ratio will belong to the option with the greatest amount of time to expiration. Occasionally, a shorter-term option will have a lower VanderPal Ratio, and if the option length is at least six months, that is the option you should use.

CHAPTER 9

Taxation

Standard stock options are treated just like investing in stocks. You receive a short-term profit on investments held for less than a year, which is treated as ordinary income. Profits on options held more than one year are taxed at the rate for long-term capital gains.

Index options receive special tax treatment per IRS Tax Code Section 1256. Investments covered by Section 1256 are subject to taxes at a rate equal to the profit being 60 percent long-term and 40 percent short-term capital gains. The special treatment of Section 1256 drops the top tax bracket effective tax rate to 28 percent, a full 12 percent lower than the ordinary income rate. You enjoy this special tax treatment even if you only hold the option for a few minutes. The effective tax rate in the 15 percent ordinary income bracket is only 6 percent.

Section 1256 has another special taxation feature known as *mark-to-market (MTM)*. Under the MTM procedure, all Section 1256 investments are evaluated for potential profit or loss at the end of the year. Any profit or loss must be reported on the year's tax return using form 6871. Even if the gain or loss was unrealized, it is treated like the option was sold at the close of the year's final trading day.

You might think it does not sound fair to be taxed on an unrealized gain and think, "What happens to me if the market tanks and the investment becomes a total loss?" Well, Section 1256 has very generous provisions for the handling of losses.

If you have a Section 1256 loss and high ordinary income for the year, you can choose to use the investment loss against this year's income and pay less tax. You also have the right to carry back the loss up to three years and apply it to any Section 1256 profits, file an amended return, and get a tax refund.

Do you have no profits in the past three years because you are new to index options trading? No problem. The rules allow you to carry the loss forward and apply it to future gains. You get to make a choice that results in you paying the lowest taxes.

Assume that you bought an SPX option for $20,000 at the beginning of 2017. At the end of the year, the option has a market value of $30,000. You have an unrealized profit of $10,000 that will be taxable. What also occurs is the tax basis for the SPX option rises to $30,000. If 2018 is a bad year for the market and you receive only $15,000 for your option, you have a $15,000 loss to apply as you see fit. It all evens out.

If you're still concerned about tax treatment for your investments, consult with your tax adviser. Tax rules change over time and may be subject to varying interpretations. Now it's time to address one of those varying interpretation questions.

Section 1256 regulations apply specifically to nonequity options. The SPX qualifies as it applies only to the movement of the index, and there is no equity ownership connected. However, the SPY is an ETF that buys stock in the S&P 500 Index components with the intent of tracking the index. There are actual equity securities involved. The question is whether options on the SPY are equity or nonequity.

The Internal Revenue Service provides no clear guidance on this matter. Thus, some brokers issue year-end tax statements treating SPY options as Section 1256 contracts and follow the MTM rule. Other brokers treat SPY options as equity options and report gains and losses only when realized. If you hold equity options a year or more, you receive full long-term capital gains treatment on equity options.

Contact your broker to determine how he or she reports gains and losses on ETF index tracking options. Your broker might give you an option to choose the reporting style. If you do not have a broker yet, make sure you ask about tax reporting styles as part of your interview process.

The best way not to worry about taxes is to employ the VanderPal Method® within a qualified tax-sheltered retirement plan. Profits within a plan, such as a self-directed IRA, accumulate tax free until you start making withdraws. Then you pay ordinary income tax only on the amount you choose to withdraw.

If you are investing using a self-directed Roth IRA, you never pay taxes on profits withdrawn after the age of 59½.

CHAPTER 10

Getting Started

Now it is time to make this real for yourself. The steps are easy.
First, you need the money.
Second, you need to decide what investment vehicles you wish to use for the principal bucket.
Third, you need to decide what percentage of interest, dividends, and principal you wish to allocate to the participation bucket.
Fourth, you need to decide which options you wish to use with the participation account.
Fifth, you need to make the investments.
It is that simple.
Well, maybe it's a little bit more difficult if you do not have a brokerage account.

Opening a Brokerage Account
The first step is finding the right broker. You have no need for a full-service, full-commission broker. You are making all your investment decisions, and there is now reason to pay higher

commissions or asset-management fees when you do not need the advice.

On the other end of the scale, you do not need to go with a lower-service, deep-discount-commission broker as there might be times when you need extra help or services that the broker does not offer. Plus, you are not trading frequently enough that the cheap commissions make that much of a difference to your returns.

The type of broker you need is what is now called a *full-service discount broker*. Brokerage commissions are low for self-directed trades, but extra services are available for extra fees. You pay for what you use. E-Trade, Charles Schwab, Fidelity Investments, Scottrade, and TD Ameritrade are some of the best-known firms.

Review each company's website to see if it offers the services you desire. Each website will be similar, but if you are buying individual bonds, some have better selections than others. Also, some of the companies compete by offering commission-free trading on certain ETFs and mutual funds. Maybe one of the brokers covers a fund you wish to use.

Make a list of questions regarding the services you desire, and make calls to see which broker best fits your needs. Remember to ask about tax treatment for the different types of options trades. Fill out the application for your favorite broker. You need approval for options trading. Some brokers build a short questionnaire into the main application, and others have a separate form. You tell them what type of options trading you plan to do. Say that you just want to buy puts and calls; approval is usually automatic.

GLOSSARY

American-Style Exercise
An option contract that may be exercised at any time between the date of purchase and the expiration date. Most exchange-traded options are American style.

Ask Price
The price at which a seller is offering to sell an option or stock.

At the Money
An option is at the money if the strike price of the option is equal to the market price of the underlying security.

Call
An option contract that gives the holder the right to buy the underlying security at a specified price for a certain, fixed period of time. *See also* Put.

Covered
A written option is considered to be covered if the writer also has an opposing market position on a share-for-share basis in the underlying security. That is, a short call is covered if the underlying stock is owned, and a short put is covered (for margin purposes) if the underlying stock is also short in the account. In addition, a short call is covered if the account is also a long call on the same security, with a striking price equal to or less than the striking price of the short call. A short put is covered if there is also a long put in the account with a striking price equal to or greater than the striking price of the short put.

Covered Call
An option strategy in which a call option is written against long stock on a share-for-share basis.

Covered Call Option Writing
A strategy in which one sells call options while simultaneously owning an equivalent position in the underlying security or strategy in which one sells put options and simultaneously is short an equivalent position in the underlying security.

Covered Put Write
A strategy in which one sells put options and simultaneously is short an equal number of shares of the underlying security.

Delta
The amount by which an option's price will change for a one-point change in price by the underlying entity. Call options have positive deltas, while put options have negative deltas. Technically, the delta is an instantaneous measure of the option's price change, so that the delta will be altered for even fractional changes by the underlying entity. See also Hedge Ratio.

European Exercise
A feature of an option that stipulates that the option may be exercised only at its expiration. Therefore, there can be no early assignment with this type of option.

Exercise
To implement the right under which the holder of an option is entitled to buy (in the case of a call) or sell (in the case of a put) the underlying security.

Expiration Date
The day on which an option contract becomes void. For stock options expiring prior to February 15, 2015, this date is the Saturday immediately following the third Friday of the expiration month. For stock options expiring on or after February 15, 2015, this date is the third Friday of the expiration month. Brokerage

firms, however, may set an earlier deadline for notification of an option buyer's intention to exercise. If Friday is a holiday, the last trading day is the preceding Thursday. *See also* Expiration Time and Automatic Exercise.

Index Option
An option whose underlying entity is an index. Most index options are cash based.

LEAPS
Long-Term Equity Anticipation Securities, or LEAPS, are long-term stock or index options. LEAPS, like all options, are available in two types, calls and puts, with expiration dates up to three years in the future.

Naked or Uncovered
A written option is considered to be uncovered if the investor does not have an offsetting position in the underlying security.

Out of the Money
A call option is out of the money if the strike price is greater than the market price of the underlying security. A put option is out of the money if the strike price is less than the market price of the underlying security.

Premium
The price of an option contract, determined in the competitive marketplace, which the buyer of the option pays to the option writer for the rights conveyed by the option contract.

Put
An option contract that gives the holder the right to sell the underlying security at a specified price for a certain fixed period of time. *See also* Call.

Volatility
A measure of the fluctuation in the market price of the underlying security. Mathematically, volatility is the annualized standard deviation of returns.
(Glossary material from the Chicago Board Options Exchange.)

About the Author

Dr. Geoffrey VanderPal, DBA, CFP®, has spent twenty-five years as a financial advisor and is a respected professor of finance at universities on four different continents.

VanderPal received his bachelor's degree with majors in finance, marketing, and management from Columbia College. He received his master's degree in business administration from Webster University and his doctorate in finance and business administration from Nova Southeastern University.

In 2002, he founded a private wealth management firm and insurance brokerage agency. He helped grow it into a multimillion-dollar business. VanderPal's business acumen has helped him succeed in several fields. He cofounded a fashion design firm and was elected village trustee in Illinois. He served as president of the Southern Nevada Financial Planning Association and as a securities arbitrator under the Financial Industry Regulatory Authority.

Made in the USA
Middletown, DE
29 January 2023